LinuxCNC Getting Started Guide

A catalogue record for this book is available from the Hong Kong Public Libraries.

Published in Hong Kong by Samurai Media Limited.

Email: info@samuraimedia.org

ISBN 978-988-8406-30-2

Background Cover Image by https://www.flickr.com/people/webtreatsetc/

Contents

The LinuxCNC Team

This handbook is a work in progress. If you are able to help with writing, editing, or graphic preparation please contact any member of the writing team or join and send an email to emc-users@lists.sourceforge.net.

Part I

Getting Started

Chapter 1

System Requirements

1.1 Minimum Requirements

The minimum system to run LinuxCNC and Ubuntu may vary depending on the exact usage. Stepper systems in general require faster threads to generate step pulses than servo systems. Using the Live-CD you can test the software before committing a computer. Keep in mind that the Latency Test numbers are more important than the processor speed for software step generation. More information on the Latency Test is here.

Additional information is on the LinuxCNC Wiki site:

Wiki.LinuxCNC.org, Hardware_Requirements

LinuxCNC and Ubuntu should run reasonably well on a computer with the following minimum hardware specification. These numbers are not the absolute minimum but will give reasonable performance for most stepper systems.

- 700 MHz x86 processor (1.2 GHz x86 processor recommended)

- 384 MB of RAM (512 MB up to 1 GB recommended)

- 8 GB hard disk

- Graphics card capable of at least 1024x768 resolution, which is not using the NVidia or ATI fglrx proprietary drivers, and which is not an onboard video chipset that shares main memory with the CPU

- A network or Internet connection (not strictly needed, but very useful for updates and for communicating with the LinuxCNC community)

Minimum hardware requirements change as Ubuntu evolves so check the Ubuntu web site for details on the LiveCD your using. Older hardware may benefit from selecting an older version of the LiveCD when available.

1.2 Problematic Hardware

1.2.1 Laptops

Laptops are not generally suited to real time software step generation. Again a Latency Test run for an extended time will give you the info you need to determine suitability.

1.2.2 Video Cards

If your installation pops up with 800 x 600 screen resolution then most likely Ubuntu does not recognize your video card or monitor. Onboard video many times causes bad real time performance.

Chapter 2

About LinuxCNC

2.1 The Software

- LinuxCNC (the Enhanced Machine Control) is a software system for computer control of machine tools such as milling machines and lathes, robots such as puma and scara and other computer controlled machines up to 9 axes.

- LinuxCNC is free software with open source code. Current versions of LinuxCNC are entirely licensed under the GNU General Public License and Lesser GNU General Public License (GPL and LGPL)

- LinuxCNC provides:

  - a graphical user interface (actually several interfaces to choose from)
  - an interpreter for *G-code* (the RS-274 machine tool programming language)
  - a realtime motion planning system with look-ahead
  - operation of low-level machine electronics such as sensors and motor drives
  - an easy to use *breadboard* layer for quickly creating a unique configuration for your machine
  - a software PLC programmable with ladder diagrams
  - easy installation with a Live-CD

- It does not provide drawing (CAD - Computer Aided Design) or G-code generation from the drawing (CAM - Computer Automated Manufacturing) functions.

- It can simultaneously move up to 9 axes and supports a variety of interfaces.

- The control can operate true servos (analog or PWM) with the feedback loop closed by the LinuxCNC software at the computer, or open loop with step-servos or stepper motors.

- Motion control features include: cutter radius and length compensation, path deviation limited to a specified tolerance, lathe threading, synchronized axis motion, adaptive feedrate, operator feed override, and constant velocity control.

- Support for non-Cartesian motion systems is provided via custom kinematics modules. Available architectures include hexapods (Stewart platforms and similar concepts) and systems with rotary joints to provide motion such as PUMA or SCARA robots.

- LinuxCNC runs on Linux using real time extensions.

2.2 The Operating System

Ubuntu has been chosen because it fits perfectly into the Open Source views of LinuxCNC:

- Ubuntu will always be free of charge, and there is no extra fee for the *enterprise edition*, we make our very best work available to everyone on the same Free terms.

- LinuxCNC is paired with the LTS versions of Ubuntu which provide support and security fixes from the Ubuntu team for 3 - 5 years.

- Ubuntu uses the very best in translations and accessibility infrastructure that the Free Software community has to offer, to make Ubuntu usable for as many people as possible.

- The Ubuntu community is entirely committed to the principles of free software development; we encourage people to use open source software, improve it and pass it on.

2.3 Getting Help

2.3.1 IRC

IRC stands for Internet Relay Chat. It is a live connection to other LinuxCNC users. The LinuxCNC IRC channel is #linuxcnc on freenode.

The simplest way to get on the IRC is to use the embedded java client on this page.

Some IRC etiquette

- Ask specific questions... Avoid questions like "Can someone help me?".
- If you're really new to all this, think a bit about your question before typing it. Make sure you give enough information so someone can solve your question.
- Have some patience when waiting for an answer, sometimes it takes a while to formulate an answer or everyone might be busy working or something.
- Set up your IRC account with your unique name so people will know who you are. If you use the java client, use the same name every time you log in. This helps people remember who you are and if you have been on before many will remember the past discussions which saves time on both ends.

Sharing Files
The most common way to share files on the IRC is to upload the file to one of the following or a similar service and paste the link:

- *For text* - http://pastebin.com/ , http://pastie.org/, https://gist.github.com/
- *For pictures* - http://imagebin.org/ , http://imgur.com/ , http://bayimg.com/
- *For files* - https://filedropper.com/ , http://filefactory.com/ , http://1fichier.com/

2.3.2 Mailing List

An Internet Mailing List is a way to put questions out for everyone on that list to see and answer at their convenience. You get better exposure to your questions on a mailing list than on the IRC but answers take longer. In a nutshell you e-mail a message to the list and either get daily digests or individual replies back depending on how you set up your account.

The emc-users mailing list

2.3.3 LinuxCNC Wiki

A Wiki site is a user maintained web site that anyone can add to or edit.

The user maintained LinuxCNC Wiki site contains a wealth of information and tips at:

http://wiki.linuxcnc.org

2.4 Getting LinuxCNC

2.4.1 Normal Download

Download the Live CD from:

the LinuxCNC homepage at www.linuxcnc.org

and follow the Download link.

2.4.2 Multi-session Download

If the file is too large to download in one session because of a bad or slow Internet connection, use *wget* to allow resuming after an interrupted download.

Wget Linux

Open a terminal window. In Ubuntu it is Applications/Accessories/Terminal. Use *cd* to change to the directory where you would like to store the ISO. Use *mkdir* to create a new directory if needed.

Note that actual file names may change so you might have to go to http://www.linuxcnc.org/ and follow the Download link to get the actual file name. In most browsers you can right click on the link and select Copy Link Location or similar, then paste the link into the terminal window with a right mouse click and select Paste.

> **Ubuntu 10.04 Lucid Lynx and LinuxCNC (current release)**
>
> To get the Ubuntu 10.04 Lucid Lynx version, copy one of these in the terminal window and press enter:
>
> For the USA mirror: wget http://linuxcnc.org/iso/ubuntu-10.04-linuxcnc3-i386.iso
>
> For the European mirror: wget http://dsplabs.upt.ro/~juve/emc/get.php?file=ubuntu-10.04-linuxcnc3-i386.iso
>
> The md5sum of the above file is: *76dc2416b917679b71255e464ede84ec*

To continue a partial download that was interrupted add the -c option to wget:

wget -c http://linuxcnc.org/iso/ubuntu-10.04-linuxcnc3-i386.iso

To stop a download use Ctrl-C or close the terminal window.

> **Ubuntu 8.04 Hardy Heron and LinuxCNC (older)**
>
> If your hardware requires an older version of Ubuntu, you can download Ubuntu 8.04 and upgrade to the latest LinuxCNC version by following the instructions on the LinuxCNC.org download page.
>
> http://linuxcnc.org/index.php/english/download

After the download is complete you will find the ISO file in the directory that you selected. Next we will burn the CD.

Wget Windows

The wget program is also available for Windows from:

http://gnuwin32.sourceforge.net/packages/wget.htm

Follow the instructions on the web page for downloading and installing the windows version of the wget program.

To run wget open a command prompt window.

In most Windows it is Programs/Accessories/Command Prompt

First you have to change to the directory where wget is installed in.

Typically it is in C:\Program Files\GnuWin32\bin so in the Command Prompt window type:

```
cd C:\Program Files\GnuWin32\bin
```

and the prompt should change to: *C:\Program Files\GnuWin32\bin>*

Type the wget command into the window and press enter as above.

2.4.3 Burning the CD

LinuxCNC is distributed as CD image files, called ISOs. To install LinuxCNC, you first need to burn the ISO file onto a CD. You need a working CD/DVD burner and an 80 minute (700 Mb) CD for this. If the CD writing fails, try writing at a slower burn speed.

Verify md5sum in Linux

Before burning a CD, it is highly recommended that you verify the md5sum (hash) of the .iso file.

Open a terminal window. In Ubuntu it is Applications/Accessories/Terminal.

Change to the directory where the ISO was downloaded to.

```
cd download_directory
```

Then run the md5sum command with the file name you saved.

```
md5sum -b ubuntu-10.04-linuxcnc1-i386.iso
```

The md5sum should print out a single line after calculating the hash. On slower computers this might take a minute or two.

```
76dc2416b917679b71255e464ede84ec *ubuntu-10.04-linuxcnc3-i386.iso
```

Now compare it to the md5sum value that it should be.

If you downloaded the md5sum as well as the iso, you can ask the md5sum program to do the checking for you. In the same directory:

```
md5sum -c ubuntu-10.04-linuxcnc1-i386.iso.md5
```

If all is well, after a short delay the terminal will print:

```
ubuntu-10.04-linuxcnc1-i386.iso: OK
```

Burning the ISO in Linux

1. Insert a blank CD into your burner. A *CD/DVD Creator* or *Choose Disc Type* window will pop up. Close this, as we will not be using it.
2. Browse to the downloaded ISO image in the file browser.
3. Right click on the ISO image file and choose Write to Disc.
4. Select the write speed. If you are burning a Ubuntu Live CD, it is recommended that you write at the lowest possible speed.
5. Start the burning process.
6. If a *choose a file name for the disc image* window pops up, just pick OK.

Verify md5sum with Windows

Before burning a CD, it is highly recommended that you verify the md5 sum (hash) of the .iso file, to ensure that you got a good download.

Windows does not come with a md5sum program. You will have to download and install one to check the md5sum. More information can be found at:

https://help.ubuntu.com/community/HowToMD5SUM

Burning the ISO in Windows

1. Download and install Infra Recorder, a free and open source image burning program: http://infrarecorder.org/
2. Insert a blank CD in the drive and select Do nothing or Cancel if an auto-run dialog pops up.
3. Open Infra Recorder, and select the *Actions* menu, then *Burn image*.

2.4.4   Testing LinuxCNC

With the Live CD in the CD/DVD drive shut down the computer then turn the computer back on. This will boot the computer from the Live CD. Once the computer has booted up you can try out LinuxCNC without installing it. You can not create custom configurations or modify most system settings like screen resolution unless you install LinuxCNC.

To try out LinuxCNC from the Applications/CNC menu pick LinuxCNC. Then select a sim configuration to try out.

To see if your computer is suitable for software step pulse generation run the Latency Test as shown here.

2.4.5   Installing LinuxCNC

If you like what you see, just click the Install icon on the desktop, answer a few questions (your name, timezone, password) and the install completes in a few minutes. Make sure you write down the name you used and the password. Once the install process is complete and you go on line the update manager will pop up and allow you to upgrade to the latest stable version of LinuxCNC.

2.4.6   Updates to LinuxCNC

With the normal install the Update Manager will notify you of updates to LinuxCNC when you go on line and allow you to easily upgrade with no Linux knowledge needed. If you want to upgrade to 10.04 from 8.04 a clean install from the Live-CD is recommended. It is OK to upgrade everything except the operating system when asked to.

Warning: Do not upgrade Ubuntu to a new but non-LTS version (like 8.04 to 8.10) as it will prevent LinuxCNC from running.

2.4.7   Install Problems

In rare cases you might have to reset the BIOS to default settings if during the Live CD install it cannot recognize the hard drive during the boot up.

Chapter 3

Updating LinuxCNC

3.1   Updating from 2.4.x to 2.5.x

As of version 2.5.0, the name of the project has changed from EMC2 to LinuxCNC. All programs with "emc" in the name have been changed to "linuxcnc" instead. All documentation has been updated.

Additionally, the name of the debian package containing the software has changed. Unfortunately this breaks automatic upgrades. To upgrade from emc2 2.4.X to linuxcnc 2.5.X, do the following:

3.1.1   On Ubuntu Lucid 10.04

First you need to tell your computer where to find the new LinuxCNC software:

- Click on the System menu in the top panel and select Administration->Software Sources.
- Select the Other Software tab.
- Select the entry that says

  ```
  http://linuxcnc.org/lucid lucid base emc2.4
  ```

  ```
  or
  ```

  ```
  http://linuxcnc.org/lucid lucid base emc2.4-sim
  ```

  ```
  and click the Edit button.
  ```

- In the Components field, change `emc2.4` to `linuxcnc2.5`, or change `emc2.4-sim` to `linuxcnc2.5-sim`.
- Click the OK button.
- Back in the Software Sources window, Other Software tab, click the Close button.
- It will pop up a window informing you that the information about available software is out-of-date. Click the Reload button.

Now your computer knows about the new software, next we need to tell it to install it:

- Click on the System menu in the top panel and select Administration->Synaptic Package Manager
- In the Quick Search bar at the top, type `linuxcnc`.
- Click the check box to mark the new linuxcnc package for installation.
- Click the Apply button, and let your computer install the new package. The old emc 2.4 package will be automatically removed to make room for the new LinuxCNC 2.5 package.

3.1.2 On Ubuntu Hardy 8.04

First you need to tell your computer where to find the new LinuxCNC software:

- Click on the System menu in the top panel and select Administration->Synaptic Package Manager

- Go to Settings->Repositories.

- Select the "Third-Party Software" tab.

- Select the entry that says

  `http://linuxcnc.org/hardy hard emc2.4`

  or

  `http://linuxcnc.org/hardy hardy emc2.4-sim`

  `and click the Edit button.`

- In the Components field, change `emc2.4` to `linuxcnc2.5` or `emc2.4-sim` to `linuxcnc2.5-sim`.

- Click the OK button.

- Back in the Software Sources window, click the Close button.

- Back in the Synaptic Package Manager window, click the Reload button.

Now your computer knows about the new software, next we need to tell it to install it:

- In the Synaptic Package Manager, click the Search button.

- In the Find dialog window that pops up, type `linuxcnc` and click the Search button.

- Click the check-box to mark the linuxcnc package for installation.

- Click the Apply button, and let your computer install the new package. The old emc 2.4 package will be automatically removed to make room for the new LinuxCNC 2.5 package.

3.2 Config changes

The user configs moved from $HOME/emc2 to $HOME/linuxcnc, so you will need to rename your directory, or move your files to the new place.

The hostmot2 watchdog in LinuxCNC 2.5 does not start running until the HAL threads start running. This means it now tolerates a timeout on the order of the servo thread period, instead of requiring a timeout that's on the order of the time between loading the driver and starting the HAL threads. This typically means a few milliseconds (a few times the servo thread period) instead of many hundreds of milliseconds. The default has been lowered from 1 second to 5 milliseconds. You generally don't need to set the hm2 watchdog timeout any more, unless you've changed your servo thread period.

The old driver for the Mesa 5i20, hal_m5i20, has been removed after being deprecated in favor of hostmot2 since early 2009 (version 2.3.) If you are still using this driver, you will need to build a new configuration using the hostmot2 driver. Pncconf may help you do this, and we have some sample configs (hm2-servo and hm2-stepper) that act as examples.

3.3   Upgrading from 2.3.x to 2.4.x

The following instructions only apply to Ubuntu 8.04 "Hardy Heron". LinuxCNC 2.4 is not available for older releases of Ubuntu.

Because there are several minor incompatibilities between 2.3.5 and 2.4.x, your existing install will not automatically be updated to 2.4.x. If you want to run 2.4.x, change to the LinuxCNC-2.4 repository by following these instructions:

run System/Administration/Synaptic Package Manager

go to Settings/Repositories

In the list of Third-Party software there should be at least two lines for linuxcnc.org.

For each of them:

- Select the line and click Edit

- On the Components line, change emc2.3 to emc2.4

- Click OK

- Close the *Software Preferences* window

- Click *Reload* as instructed

- Click *Mark All Upgrades*

> **Mesa card and hostmot2 users:**
>
> If you use a mesa card, find the proper hostmot2-firmware package for your card and mark it for installation. Hint: do a search for *hostmot2-firmware* in the synaptic package manager.

- Click *Apply*

3.4   Changes between 2.3.x and 2.4.x

Once you have done the upgrade, update any custom configurations by following these instructions:

3.4.1   emc.nml changes (2.3.x to 2.4.x)

For configurations that have not customized emc.nml, remove or comment out the inifile line NML_FILE = emc.nml. This will cause the most up to date version of emc.nml to be used.

For configurations that have customized emc.nml, a change similar to this one is required.

Failure to do this can cause an error like this one:

```
libnml/buffer/physmem.cc 143: PHYSMEM_HANDLE:
Can't write 10748 bytes at offset 60 from buffer of size 10208.
```

3.4.2   tool table changes (2.3.x to 2.4.x)

The format of the tool table has been changed incompatibly. The documentation shows the new format. The tool table will automatically be converted to the new format.

3.4.3 hostmot2 firmware images (2.3.x to 2.4.x)

The hostmot2 firmware images are now a separate package. You can:

- Continue using an already-installed *emc2-firmware-mesa-** 2.3.x package

- Install the new packages from the synaptic package manager. The new packages are named *hostmot2-firmware-**

- Download the firmware images as tar files from http://emergent.unpy.net/01267622561 and install them manually

Chapter 4

Stepper Quickstart

This section assumes you have done a standard install from the Live CD. After installation it is recommended that you connect the computer to the Internet and wait for the update manager to pop up and get the latest updates for LinuxCNC and Ubuntu before continuing. For more complex installations see the Integrator Manual.

4.1 Latency Test

The Latency Test determines how late your computer processor is in responding to a request. Some hardware can interrupt the processing which could cause missed steps when running a CNC machine. This is the first thing you need to do. Follow the instructions here to run the latency test.

4.2 Sherline

If you have a Sherline several predefined configurations are provided. This is on the main menu CNC/EMC then pick the Sherline configuration that matches yours and save a copy.

4.3 Xylotex

If you have a Xylotex you can skip the following sections and go straight to the Stepper Config Wizard. LinuxCNC has provided quick setup for the Xylotex machines.

4.4 Machine Information

Gather the information about each axis of your machine.

Drive timing is in nano seconds. If you're unsure about the timing many popular drives are included in the stepper configuration wizard. Note some newer Gecko drives have different timing than the original one. A list is also on the user maintained LinuxCNC wiki site of more drives.

Axis	Drive Type	Step Time ns	Step Space ns	Dir. Hold ns	Dir. Setup ns
X					
Y					
Z					

4.5   Pinout Information

Gather the information about the connections from your machine to the PC parallel port.

Output Pin	Typ. Function	If Different	Input Pin	Typ. Function	If Different
1	E-Stop Out		10	X Limit/Home	
2	X Step		11	Y Limit/Home	
3	X Direction		12	Z Limit/Home	
4	Y Step		13	A Limit/Home	
5	Y Direction		15	Probe In	
6	Z Step				
7	Z Direction				
8	A Step				
9	A Direction				
14	Spindle CW				
16	Spindle PWM				
17	Amplifier Enable				

Note any pins not used should be set to Unused in the drop down box. These can always be changed later by running Stepconf again.

4.6   Mechanical Information

Gather information on steps and gearing. The result of this is steps per user unit which is used for SCALE in the .ini file.

Axis	Steps/Rev.	Micro Steps	Motor Teeth	Leadscrew Teeth	Leadscrew Pitch
X					
Y					
Z					

- *Steps per revolution* - is how many stepper-motor-steps it takes to turn the stepper motor one revolution. Typical is 200.

- *Micro Steps* - is how many steps the drive needs to move the stepper motor one full step. If microstepping is not used, this number will be 1. If microstepping is used the value will depend on the stepper drive hardware.

- *Motor Teeth and Leadscrew Teeth* - is if you have some reduction (gears, chain, timing belt, etc.) between the motor and the leadscrew. If not, then set these both to 1.

- *Leadscrew Pitch* - is how much movement occurs (in user units) in one leadscrew turn. If you're setting up in inches then it is inches per turn. If you're setting up in millimeters then it is millimeters per turn.

The net result you're looking for is how many CNC-output-steps it takes to move one user unit (inches or mm).

Example 4.1 Units inches

```
Stepper          = 200 steps per revolution
Drive            =  10 micro steps per step
Motor Teeth      =  20
Leadscrew Teeth  =  40
Leadscrew Pitch  =   0.2000 inches per turn
```

From the above information, the leadscrew moves 0.200 inches per turn. - The motor turns 2.000 times per 1 leadscrew turn. - The drive takes 10 microstep inputs to make the stepper step once. - The drive needs 2000 steps to turn the stepper one revolution. So the scale needed is:

$$\frac{200\,full\,steps}{1\,rev} \times \frac{8\,microsteps}{1\,step} \times \frac{2\,revs}{1\,leadscrew\,rev} \times \frac{1\,leadscrew\,rev}{0.200\,inch} = \frac{20,000\,steps}{1\,inch}$$

Example 4.2 Units mm

```
Stepper          = 200 steps per revolution
Drive            =   8 micro steps per step
Motor Teeth      =  30
Leadscrew Teeth  =  90
Leadscrew Pitch  =   5.00 mm per turn
```

From the above information: - The leadscrew moves 5.00 mm per turn. - The motor turns 3.000 times per 1 leadscrew turn. - The drive takes 8 microstep inputs to make the stepper step once. - The drive needs 1600 steps to turn the stepper one revolution. So the scale needed is:

$$\frac{200\,full\,steps}{1\,rev} \times \frac{8\,microsteps}{1\,step} \times \frac{3\,revs}{1\,leadscrew\,rev} \times \frac{1\,leadscrew\,rev}{5.00mm} = \frac{960\,steps}{1\,mm}$$

Chapter 5

Stepper Configuration Wizard

LinuxCNC is capable of controlling a wide range of machinery using many different hardware interfaces.

Stepconf is a program that generates configuration files for LinuxCNC for a specific class of CNC machine: those that are controlled via a *standard parallel port*, and controlled by signals of type *step & direction*.

Stepconf is installed when you install LinuxCNC and is in the CNC menu.

Stepconf places a file in the linuxcnc/config directory to store the choices for each configuration you create. When you change something, you need to pick the file that matches your configuration name. The file extension is .stepconf.

The Stepconf Wizard needs at least 800 x 600 screen resolution to see the buttons on the bottom of the pages.

Step by Step Instructions

5.1   Entry Page

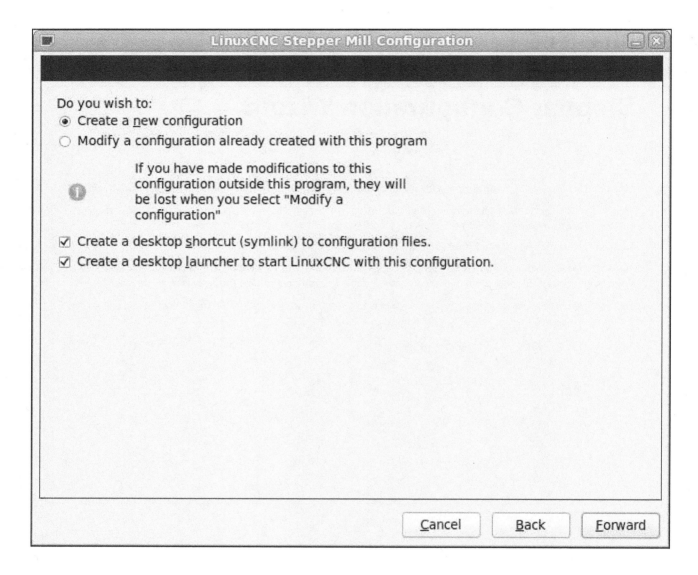

Figure 5.1: Entry Page

- *Create New* - Creates a fresh configuration.

- *Modify* - Modify an existing configuration. After selecting this a file picker pops up so you can select the .stepconf file for modification. If you made any modifications to the main .hal or the .ini file these will be lost. Modifications to custom.hal and custom_postgui.hal will not be changed by the Stepconf Wizard.

- *Create Desktop Shortcut* - This will place a link on your desktop to the files.

- *Create Desktop Launcher* - This will place a launcher on your desktop to start your application.

5.2   Basic Information

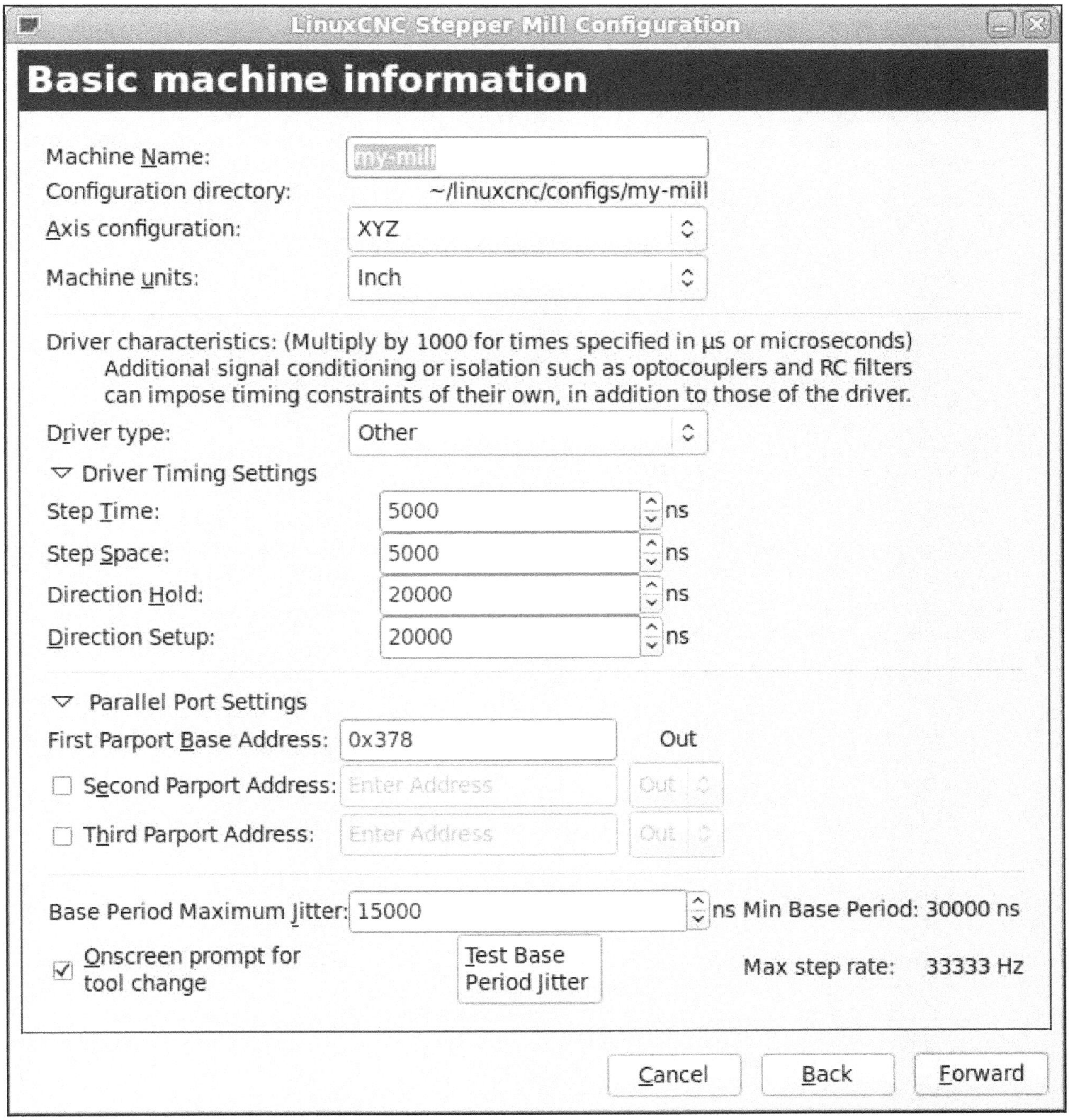

Figure 5.2: Basic Information Page

- *Machine Name* - Choose a name for your machine. Use only uppercase letters, lowercase letters, digits, - and _.

- *Axis Configuration* - Choose XYZ (Mill), XYZA (4-axis mill) or XZ (Lathe).

- *Machine Units* - Choose Inch or mm. All subsequent entries will be in the chosen units

- *Driver Type* - If you have one of the stepper drivers listed in the pull down box, choose it. Otherwise, select *Other* and find the timing values in your driver's data sheet and enter them as *nano seconds* in the *Driver Timing Settings*. If the data sheet gives a value in microseconds, multiply by 1000. For example, enter 4.5us as 4500ns.

A list of some popular drives, along with their timing values, is on the LinuxCNC.org Wiki under Stepper Drive Timing.

Additional signal conditioning or isolation such as optocouplers and RC filters on break out boards can impose timing constraints of their own, in addition to those of the driver. You may find it necessary to add some time to the drive requirements to allow for this.

The LinuxCNC Configuration Selector has configs for Sherline already configured.

- *Step Time* - How long the step pulse is *on* in nano seconds. If your not sure about this setting a value of 10,000 will work with most drives.

- *Step Space* - Minimum time between step pulses in nano seconds. If your not sure about this setting a value of 10,000 will work with most drives.

- *Direction Hold* - How long the direction pin is held after a change of direction in nanoseconds. If your not sure about this setting a value of 200,000 will work with most drives.

- *Direction Setup* - How long before a direction change after the last step pulse in nanoseconds. If your not sure about this setting a value of 200,000 will work with most drives.

- *First Parport* - Usually the default of 0x378 is correct.

- *Second Parport* - If you need to specify additional parallel ports enter the address and the type. For information on finding the address of PCI parallel ports see the Port Address in the Integrator Manual. (Try 0x278 or 0x3BC first.)

- *Base Period Maximum Jitter* - Enter the result of the Latency Test here. To run a latency test press the *Test Base Period Jitter* button. See the Latency Test section for more details.

- *Max Step Rate* -Stepconf automatically calculates the Max Step Rate based on the driver characteristics entered and the latency test result.

- *Min Base Period* - Stepconf automatically determines the Min Base Period based on the driver characteristics entered and latency test result.

- *Onscreen Prompt For Tool Change* - If this box is checked, LinuxCNC will pause and prompt you to change the tool when *M6* is encountered. This feature is usually only useful if you have presettable tools.

5.3 Latency Test

While the test is running, you should *abuse* the computer. Move windows around on the screen. Surf the web. Copy some large files around on the disk. Play some music. Run an OpenGL program such as glxgears. The idea is to put the PC through its paces while the latency test checks to see what the worst case numbers are. Run the test at least a few minutes. The longer you run the test the better it will be at catching events that might occour at less frequent intervals. This is a test for your computer only, so no hardware needs to be connected to run the test.

Warning
Do not attempt run LinuxCNC while the latency test is running.

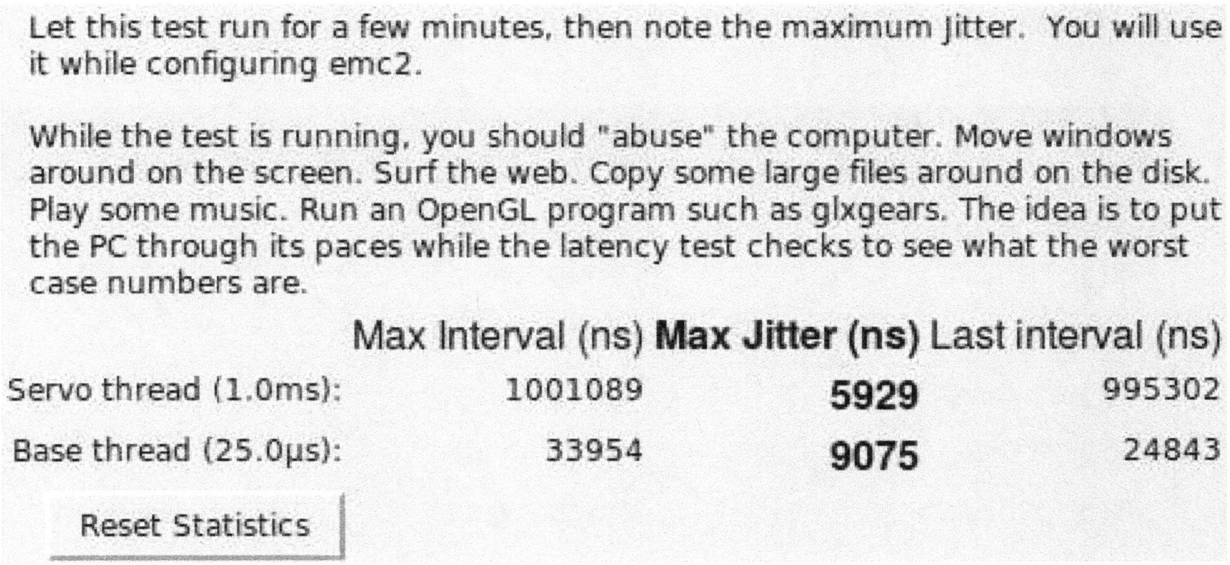

Let this test run for a few minutes, then note the maximum jitter. You will use it while configuring emc2.

While the test is running, you should "abuse" the computer. Move windows around on the screen. Surf the web. Copy some large files around on the disk. Play some music. Run an OpenGL program such as glxgears. The idea is to put the PC through its paces while the latency test checks to see what the worst case numbers are.

	Max Interval (ns)	**Max Jitter (ns)**	Last interval (ns)
Servo thread (1.0ms):	1001089	**5929**	995302
Base thread (25.0μs):	33954	**9075**	24843

Reset Statistics

Figure 5.3: Latency Test

Latency is how long it takes the PC to stop what it is doing and respond to an external request. In our case, the request is the periodic *heartbeat* that serves as a timing reference for the step pulses. The lower the latency, the faster you can run the heartbeat, and the faster and smoother the step pulses will be.

Latency is far more important than CPU speed. The CPU isn't the only factor in determining latency. Motherboards, video cards, USB ports, SMI issues, and a number of other things can hurt the latency.

Troubleshooting SMI Issues (LinuxCNC.org Wiki)

Fixing Realtime problems caused by SMI on Ubuntu

http://wiki.linuxcnc.org/cgi-bin/wiki.pl?FixingSMIIssues

The important numbers are the *max jitter*. In the example above 9075 nanoseconds, or 9.075 microseconds, is the highest jitter. Record this number, and enter it in the Base Period Maximum Jitter box.

If your Max Jitter number is less than about 15-20 microseconds (15000-20000 nanoseconds), the computer should give very nice results with software stepping. If the max latency is more like 30-50 microseconds, you can still get good results, but your maximum step rate might be a little disappointing, especially if you use microstepping or have very fine pitch leadscrews. If the numbers are 100 us or more (100,000 nanoseconds), then the PC is not a good candidate for software stepping. Numbers over 1 millisecond (1,000,000 nanoseconds) mean the PC is not a good candidate for LinuxCNC, regardless of whether you use software stepping or not.

5.4   Parallel Port Setup

Parallel Port Setup

Outputs (PC to Mill):		Invert	Inputs (Mill to PC):		Invert
Pin 1:	ESTOP Out ⇕	☐	Pin 10:	Unused ⇕	☐
Pin 2:	X Step ⇕	☐	Pin 11:	Unused ⇕	☐
Pin 3:	X Direction ⇕	☐	Pin 12:	Unused ⇕	☐
Pin 4:	Y Step ⇕	☐	Pin 13:	Unused ⇕	☐
Pin 5:	Y Direction ⇕	☐	Pin 15:	Unused ⇕	☐
Pin 6:	Z Step ⇕	☐			
Pin 7:	Z Direction ⇕	☐			
Pin 8:	A Step ⇕	☐			
Pin 9:	A Direction ⇕	☐			
Pin 14:	Spindle CW ⇕	☐	Output pinout presets:		
Pin 16:	Spindle PWM ⇕	☐	Sherline Outputs		
Pin 17:	Amplifier Enable ⇕	☐	Xylotex Outputs		

Cancel   Back   Forward

Figure 5.4: Parallel Port Setup Page

For each pin, choose the signal which matches your parallel port pinout. Turn on the *invert* check box if the signal is inverted (0V for true/active, 5V for false/inactive).

- *Output pinout presets* - Automatically set pins 2 through 9 according to the Sherline standard (Direction on pins 2, 4, 6, 8) or the Xylotex standard (Direction on pins 3, 5, 7, 9).

- *Inputs and Outputs* - If the input or output is not used set the option to *Unused*.

- *External E Stop* - This can be selected from an input pin drop down box. A typical E Stop chain uses all normally closed contacts.

- *Homing & Limit Switches* - These can be selected from an input pin drop down box for most configurations.

- *Charge Pump* - If your driver board requires a charge pump signal select Charge Pump from the drop down list for the output pin you wish to connect to your charge pump input. The charge pump output is connected to the base thread by Stepconf. The charge pump output will be about 1/2 of the maximum step rate shown on the Basic Machine Configuration page.

5.5 Axis Configuration

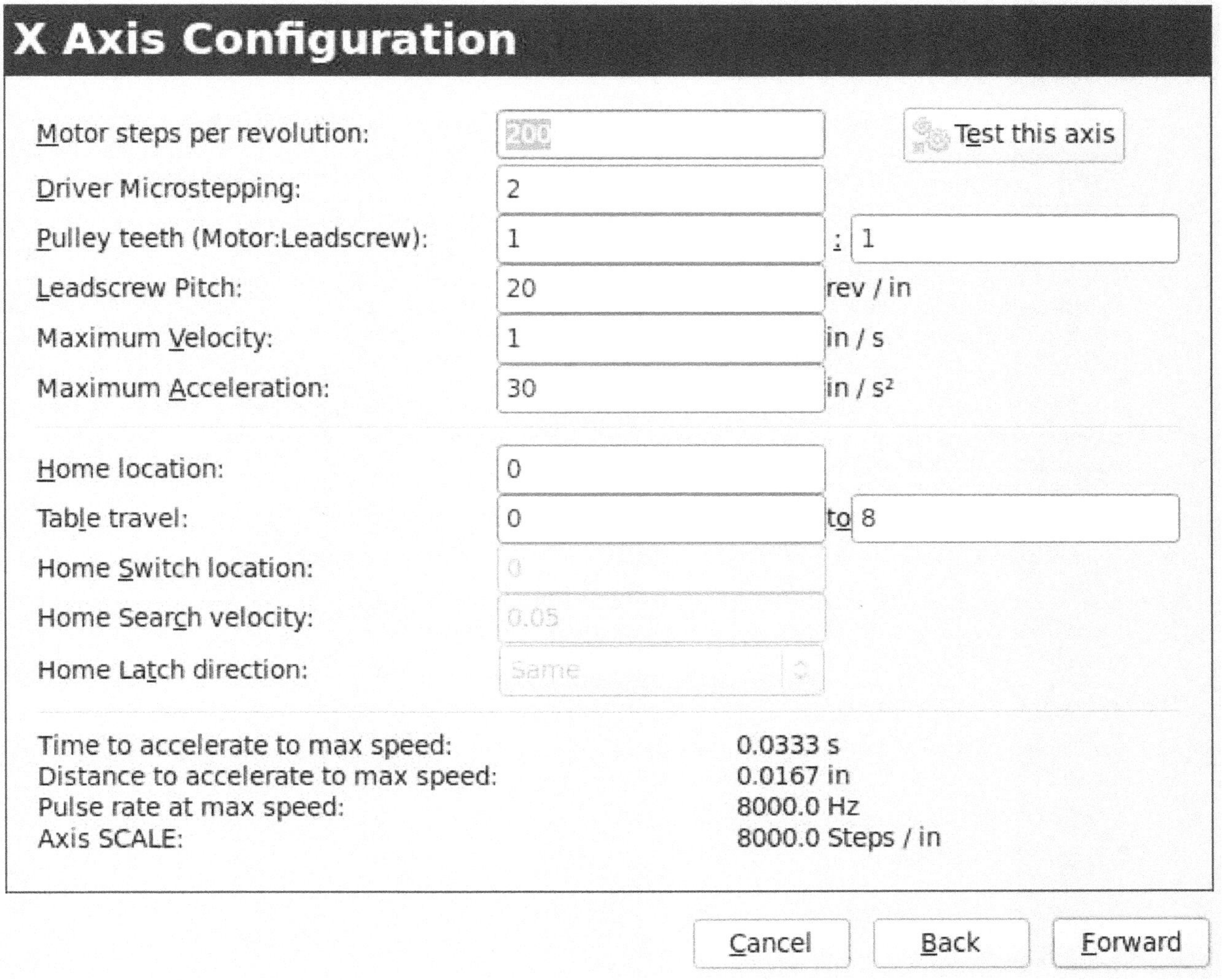

X Axis Configuration

Motor steps per revolution:	200		Test this axis
Driver Microstepping:	2		
Pulley teeth (Motor:Leadscrew):	1	:	1
Leadscrew Pitch:	20	rev / in	
Maximum Velocity:	1	in / s	
Maximum Acceleration:	30	in / s²	

Home location:	0		
Table travel:	0	to	8
Home Switch location:	0		
Home Search velocity:	0.05		
Home Latch direction:	Same		

Time to accelerate to max speed:	0.0333 s
Distance to accelerate to max speed:	0.0167 in
Pulse rate at max speed:	8000.0 Hz
Axis SCALE:	8000.0 Steps / in

Cancel   Back   Forward

Figure 5.5: Axis Configuration Page

- *Motor Steps Per Revolution* - The number of full steps per motor revolution. If you know how many degrees per step the motor is (e.g., 1.8 degree), then divide 360 by the degrees per step to find the number of steps per motor revolution.

- *Driver Microstepping* - The amount of microstepping performed by the driver. Enter *2* for half-stepping.

- *Pulley Ratio* - If your machine has pulleys between the motor and leadscrew, enter the ratio here. If not, enter *1:1*.

- *Leadscrew Pitch* - Enter the pitch of the leadscrew here. If you chose *Inch* units, enter the number of threads per inch If you chose *mm* units, enter the number of millimeters per revolution (e.g., enter 2 for 2mm/rev). If the machine travels in the wrong direction, enter a negative number here instead of a positive number, or invert the direction pin for the axis.

- *Maximum Velocity* -Enter the maximum velocity for the axis in units per second.

- *Maximum Acceleration* - The correct values for these items can only be determined through experimentation. See Finding Maximum Velocity to set the speed and Finding Maximum Acceleration to set the acceleration.

- *Home Location* - The position the machine moves to after completing the homing procedure for this axis. For machines without home switches, this is the location the operator manually moves the machine to before pressing the Home button. If you combine the home and limit switches you must move off of the switch to the home position or you will get a joint limit error.

- *Table Travel* - The range of travel for that axis based on the machine origin. The home location must be inside the *Table Travel* and not equal to one of the Table Travel values.

- *Home Switch Location* - The location at which the home switch trips or releases reletive to the machine origin. This item and the two below only appear when Home Switches were chosen in the Parallel Port Pinout. If you combine home and limit switches the home switch location can not be the same as the home position or you will get a joint limit error.

- *Home Search Velocity* - The velocity to use when searching for the home switch. If the switch is near the end of travel, this velocity must be chosen so that the axis can decelerate to a stop before hitting the end of travel. If the switch is only closed for a short range of travel (instead of being closed from its trip point to one end of travel), this velocity must be chosen so that the axis can decelerate to a stop before the switch opens again, and homing must always be started from the same side of the switch. If the machine moves the wrong direction at the beginning of the homing procedure, negate the value of *Home Search Velocity*.

- *Home Latch Direction* - Choose *Same* to have the axis back off the switch, then approach it again at a very low speed. The second time the switch closes, the home position is set. Choose *Opposite* to have the axis back off the switch and when the switch opens, the home position is set.

- *Time to accelerate to max speed* - Time to reach maximum speed calculated from *Max Acceleration* and *Max Velocity*.

- *Distance to accelerate to max speed* - Distance to reach maximum speed from a standstill.

- *Pulse rate at max speed* - Information computed based on the values entered above. The greatest *Pulse rate at max speed* determines the *BASE_PERIOD*. Values above 20000Hz may lead to slow response time or even lockups (the fastest usable pulse rate varies from computer to computer)

- *Axis SCALE* - The number that will be used in the ini file [SCALE] setting. This is how many steps per user unit.

- *Test this axis* - This will open a window to allow testing for each axis. This can be used after filling out all the information for this axis.

5.5.1 Test This Axis

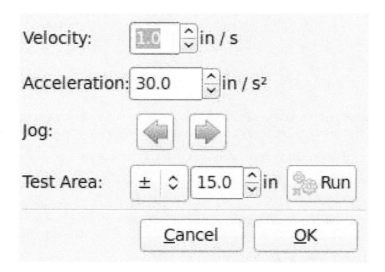

Figure 5.6: Test This Axis

Test this axis is a basic tester that only outputs step and direction signals to try different values for acceleration and velocity.

 Important

In order to use test this axis you have to manually enable the axis if this is required. If your driver has a charge pump you will have to bypass it. Test this axis does not react to limit switch inputs. Use with caution.

5.5.1.1 Finding Maximum Velocity

Begin with a low Acceleration (for example, `2 inches/s`^{2} or `50 mm/s`^{2}) and the velocity you hope to attain. Using the buttons provided, jog the axis to near the center of travel. Take care because with a low acceleration value, it can take a surprising distance for the axis to decelerate to a stop.

After gaging the amount of travel available, enter a safe distance in Test Area, keeping in mind that after a stall the motor may next start to move in an unexpected direction. Then click Run. The machine will begin to move back and forth along this axis. In this test, it is important that the combination of Acceleration and Test Area allow the machine to reach the selected Velocity and *cruise* for at least a short distance — the more distance, the better this test is. The formula `d =0.5 * v * v/a` gives the minimum distance required to reach the specified velocity with the given acceleration. If it is convenient and safe to do so, push the table against the direction of motion to simulate cutting forces. If the machine stalls, reduce the speed and start the test again.

If the machine did not obviously stall, click the *Run* button off. The axis now returns to the position where it started. If the position is incorrect, then the axis stalled or lost steps during the test. Reduce Velocity and start the test again.

If the machine doesn't move, stalls, or loses steps, no matter how low you turn Velocity, verify the following:

- Correct step waveform timings

- Correct pinout, including *Invert* on step pins

- Correct, well-shielded cabling

- Physical problems with the motor, motor coupling, leadscrew, etc.

Once you have found a speed at which the axis does not stall or lose steps during this testing procedure, reduce it by 10% and use that as the axis *Maximum Velocity*.

5.5.1.2 Finding Maximum Acceleration

With the Maximum Velocity you found in the previous step, enter the acceleration value to test. Using the same procedure as above, adjust the Acceleration value up or down as necessary. In this test, it is important that the combination of Acceleration and Test Area allow the machine to reach the selected Velocity. Once you have found a value at which the axis does not stall or lose steps during this testing procedure, reduce it by 10% and use that as the axis Maximum Acceleration.

5.6   Spindle Configuration

Spindle Configuration

PWM Rate:	100	Hz Enter 0 Hz for "PDM" mode
Calibration:		
Speed 1:	100	PWM 1: 0.2
Speed 2:	800	PWM 2: 0.8

Cycles per revolution: 100

Cancel   Back   Forward

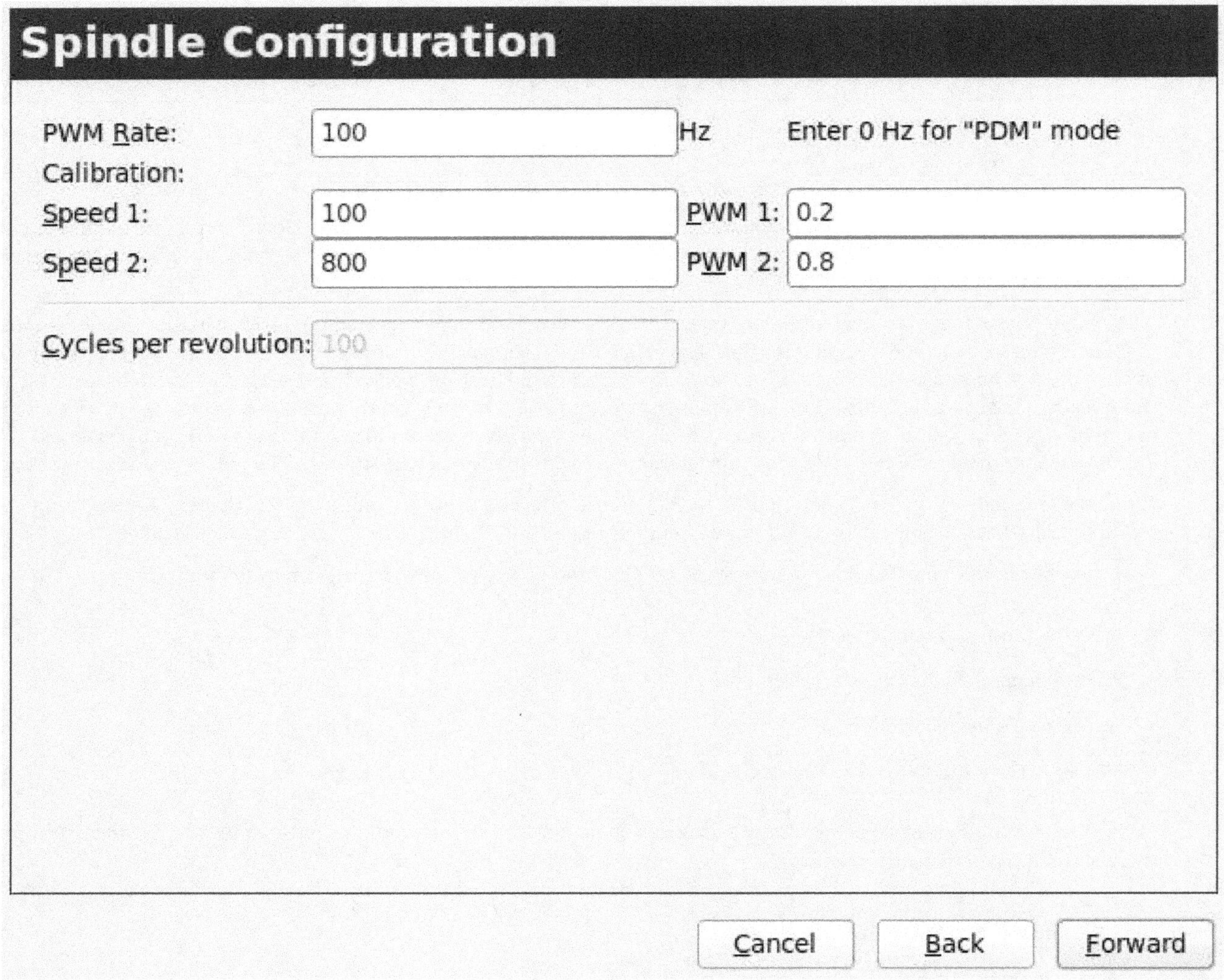

Figure 5.7: Spindle Configuration Page

This page only appears when *Spindle PWM* is chosen in the *Parallel Port Pinout* page for one of the outputs.

5.6.1   Spindle Speed Control

If *Spindle PWM* appears on the pinout, the following information should be entered:

- *PWM Rate* - The *carrier frequency* of the PWM signal to the spindle. Enter *0* for PDM mode, which is useful for generating an analog control voltage. Refer to the documentation for your spindle controller for the appropriate value.

- *Speed 1 and 2, PWM 1 and 2* - The generated configuration file uses a simple linear relationship to determine the PWM value for a given RPM value. If the values are not known, they can be determined. For more information see Determining Spindle Calibration.

5.6.2 Spindle-synchronized motion

When the appropriate signals from a spindle encoder are connected to LinuxCNC via HAL, LinuxCNC supports lathe threading. These signals are:

- *Spindle Index* - Is a pulse that occurs once per revolution of the spindle.

- *Spindle Phase A* - This is a pulse that occurs in multiple equally-spaced locations as the spindle turns.

- *Spindle Phase B (optional)* - This is a second pulse that occurs, but with an offset from Spindle Phase A. The advantages to using both A and B are direction sensing, increased noise immunity, and increased resolution.

If *Spindle Phase A* and *Spindle Index* appear on the pinout, the following information should be entered:

- *Cycles per revolution* - The number of cycles of the *Spindle A* signal during one revolution of the spindle. This option is only enabled when an input has been set to *Spindle Phase A*

- *Maximum speed in thread* - The maximum spindle speed used in threading. For a high spindle RPM or a spindle encoder with high resolution, a low value of *BASE_PERIOD* is required.

5.6.3 Determining Spindle Calibration

Enter the following values in the Spindle Configuration page:

Speed 1:	0	PWM 1:	0
Speed 2:	1000	PWM 2:	1

Finish the remaining steps of the configuration process, then launch LinuxCNC with your configuration. Turn the machine on and select the MDI tab. Start the spindle turning by entering: *M3 S100*. Change the spindle speed by entering a different S-number: *S800*. Valid numbers (at this point) range from 1 to 1000.

For two different S-numbers, measure the actual spindle speed in RPM. Record the S-numbers and actual spindle speeds. Run Stepconf again. For *Speed* enter the measured speed, and for *PWM* enter the S-number divided by 1000.

Because most spindle drivers are somewhat nonlinear in their response curves, it is best to:

- Make sure the two calibration speeds are not too close together in RPM

- Make sure the two calibration speeds are in the range of speeds you will typically use while milling

For instance, if your spindle will go from 0 RPM to 8000 RPM, but you generally use speeds from 400 RPM (10%) to 4000 RPM (100%), then find the PWM values that give 1600 RPM (40%) and 2800 RPM (70%).

5.7   Advanced Configuration Options

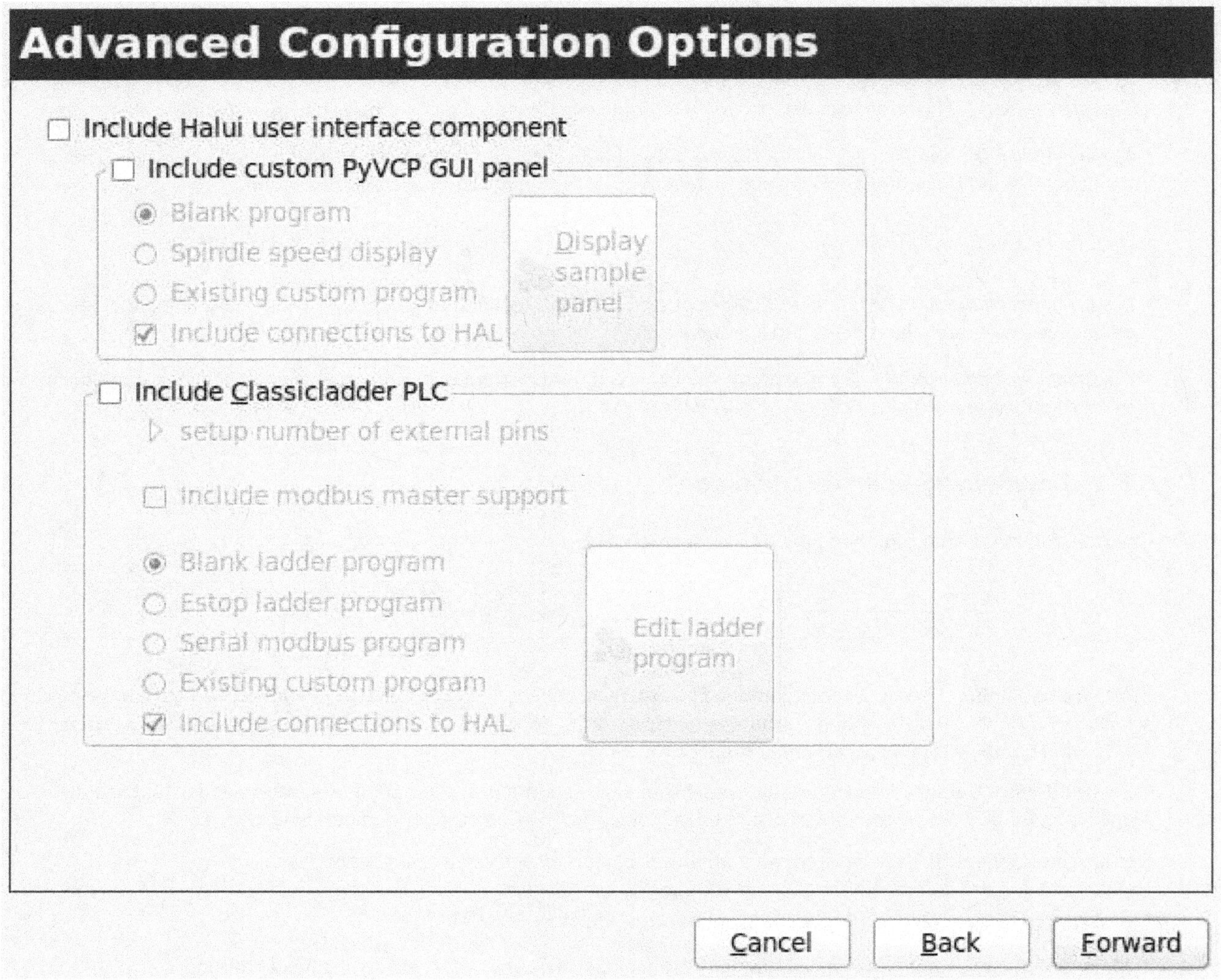

Figure 5.8: Advanced Configuration

- *Include Halui* - This will add the Halui user interface component. See the Integrator Manual for more information on Halui.

- *Include pyVCP* - This option adds the pyVCP panel base file or a sample file to work on. See the Integrator Manual for more information on pyVCP.

- *Include ClassicLadder PLC* - This option will add the ClassicLadder PLC (Programmable Logic Controller). See the Integrator Manual for more information on ClassicLadder.

5.8   Machine Configuration Complete

Click *Apply* to write the configuration files. Later, you can re-run this program and tweak the settings you entered before.

5.9 Axis Travel, Home Location, and Home Switch Location

For each axis, there is a limited range of travel. The physical end of travel is called the *hard stop*.

Before the *hard stop* there is a *limit switch*. If the limit switch is encountered during normal operation, LinuxCNC shuts down the motor amplifier. The distance between the *hard stop* and *limit switch* must be long enough to allow an unpowered motor to coast to a stop.

Before the *limit switch* there is a *soft limit*. This is a limit enforced in software after homing. If a MDI command or g code program would pass the soft limit, it is not executed. If a jog would pass the soft limit, it is terminated at the soft limit.

The *home switch* can be placed anywhere within the travel (between hard stops). As long as external hardware does not deactivate the motor amplifiers when the limit switch is reached, one of the limit switches can be used as a home switch.

The *zero position* is the location on the axis that is 0 in the machine coordinate system. Usually the *zero position* will be within the *soft limits*. On lathes, constant surface speed mode requires that machine *X=0* correspond to the center of spindle rotation when no tool offset is in effect.

The *home position* is the location within travel that the axis will be moved to at the end of the homing sequence. This value must be within the *soft limits*. In particular, the *home position* should never be exactly equal to a *soft limit*.

5.9.1 Operating without Limit Switches

A machine can be operated without limit switches. In this case, only the soft limits stop the machine from reaching the hard stop. Soft limits only operate after the machine has been homed.

5.9.2 Operating without Home Switches

A machine can be operated without home switches. If the machine has limit switches, but no home switches, it is best to use a limit switch as the home switch (e.g., choose *Minimum Limit + Home X* in the pinout). If the machine has no switches at all, or the limit switches cannot be used as home switches for another reason, then the machine must be homed *by eye* or by using match marks. Homing by eye is not as repeatable as homing to switches, but it still allows the soft limits to be useful.

5.9.3 Home and Limit Switch wiring options

The ideal wiring for external switches would be one input per switch. However, the PC parallel port only offers a total of 5 inputs, while there are as many as 9 switches on a 3-axis machine. Instead, multiple switches are wired together in various ways so that a smaller number of inputs are required.

The figures below show the general idea of wiring multiple switches to a single input pin. In each case, when one switch is actuated, the value seen on INPUT goes from logic HIGH to LOW. However, LinuxCNC expects a TRUE value when a switch is closed, so the corresponding *Invert* box must be checked on the pinout configuration page. The pull up resistor show in the diagrams pulls the input high until the connection to ground is made and then the input goes low. Otherwise the input might float between on and off when the circuit is open. Typically for a parallel port you might use 47k.

Normally Closed Switches Wiring N/C switches in series (simplified diagram)

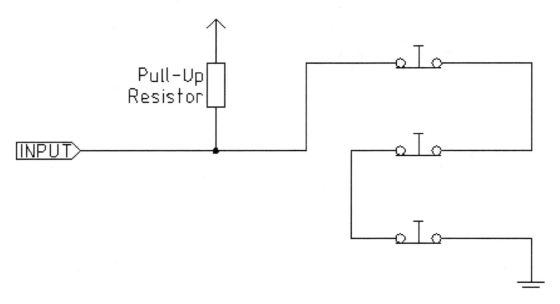

Normally Open Switches Wiring N/O switches in parallel (simplified diagram)

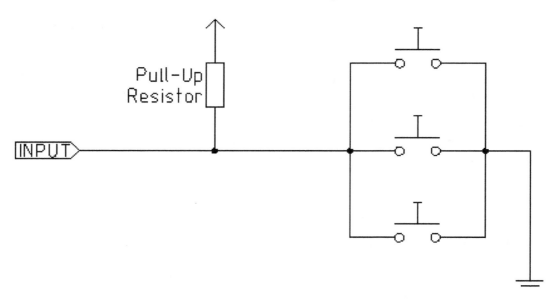

The following combinations of switches are permitted in Stepconf:

- Combine home switches for all axes

- Combine limit switches for all axes

- Combine both limit switches for one axis

- Combine both limit switches and the home switch for one axis

- Combine one limit switch and the home switch for one axis

Chapter 6

Mesa Configuration Wizard

PNCconf is made to help build configurations that utilize specific Mesa *Anything I/O* products.

It can configure closed loop servo systems or hardware stepper systems. It uses a similar *wizard* approach as Stepconf (used for software stepping, parallel port driven systems).

PNCconf is still in a development stage (Beta) so there are some bugs and lacking features. Please report bugs and suggestions to the LinuxCNC forum page or mail-list.

There are two trains of thought when using PNCconf:

One is to use PNCconf to always configure your system - if you decide to change options, reload PNCconf and allow it to configure the new options. This will work well if your machine is fairly standard and you can use custom files to add non standard features. PNCconf tries to work with you in this regard.

The other is to use PNCconf to build a config that is close to what you want and then hand edit everything to tailor it to your needs. This would be the choice if you need extensive modifications beyond PNCconf's scope or just want to tinker with / learn about LinuxCNC

You navigate the wizard pages with the forward, back, and cancel buttons there is also a help button that gives some help information about the pages, diagrams and an output page.

Tip
PNCconf's help page should have the most up to date info and has additional details.

Step by Step Instructions

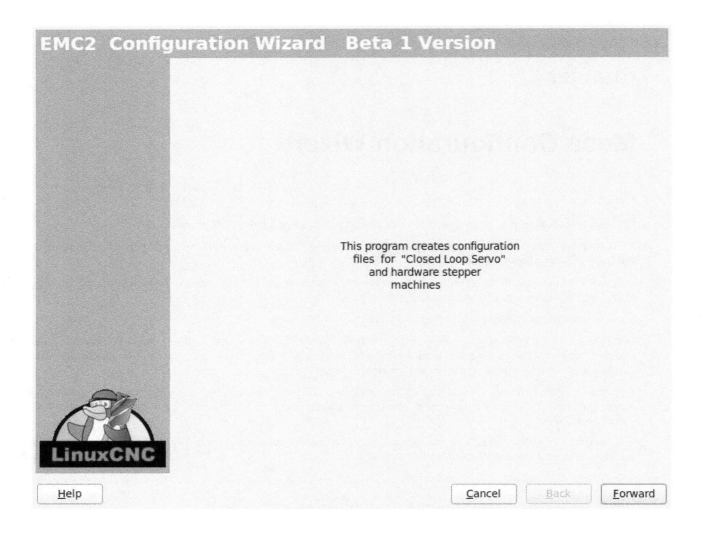

Figure 6.1: PnCConf Splash

6.1   Create or Edit

This allows you to select a previously saved configuration or create a new one. If you pick *Modify a configuration* and then press next a file selection box will show. Pncconf preselects your last saved file. Choose the the config you wish to edit. It also allows you to select desktop shortcut / launcher options. A desktop shortcut will place a folder icon on the desktop that points to your new configuration files. Otherwise you would have to look in your home folder under emc2/configs.

A Desktop launcher will add an icon to the desktop for starting your config directly. You can also launch it under Applications/cnc/emc2 and selecting your config name.

6.2 Basic Machine Information

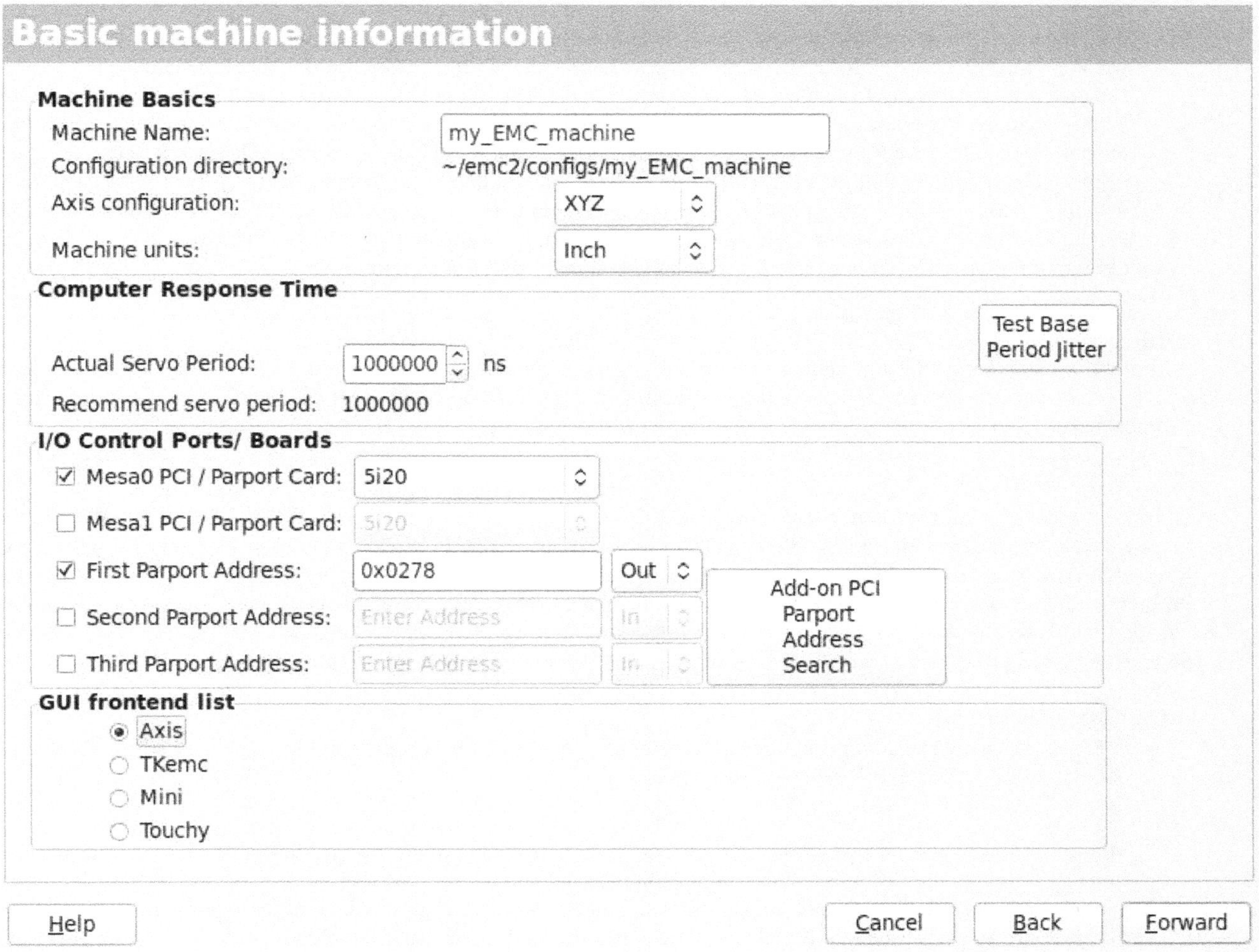

Figure 6.2: PnCConf Basic

Machine Basics

If you use a name with spaces PNCconf will replace the spaces with underscore (as a loose rule Linux doesn't like spaces in names) Pick an axis configuration - this selects what type of machine you are building and what axes are available. The Machine units selector allows data entry of metric or imperial units in the following pages.

Tip
Defaults are not converted when using metric so make sure they are sane values!

Computer Response Time

The servo period sets the heart beat of the system. Latency refers to the amount of time the computer can be longer then that period. Just like a railroad, LinuxCNC requires everything on a very tight and consistent time line or bad things happen. LinuxCNC requires and uses a *real time* operating system, which just means it has a low latency (lateness) response time when LinuxCNC requires its calculations and when doing LinuxCNCs calculations it cannot be interrupted by lower priority requests (such as user input to screen buttons or drawing etc).

Testing the latency is very important and a key thing to check early. Luckily by using the Mesa card to do the work that requires the fastest response time (encoder counting and PWM generation) we can endure a lot more latency then if we used the parallel port for these things. The standard test in LinuxCNC is checking the BASE period latency (even though we are not using a base period). If you press the *test base period jitter* button, this launches the latency test window (you can also load this directly from the applications/cnc panel). The test mentions to run it for a few minutes but the longer the better. consider 15 minutes a bare minimum and overnight even better. At this time use the computer to load things, use the net, use USB etc we want to know the worst case latency and to find out if any particular activity hurts our latency. We need to look at base period jitter. Anything under 20000 is excellent - you could even do fast software stepping with the machine 20000 - 50000 is still good for software stepping and fine for us. 50000 - 100000 is really not that great but could still be used with hardware cards doing the fast response stuff. So anything under 100000 is useable to us. If the latency is disappointing or you get a bad hiccup periodically you may still be able to improve it.

Tip

There is a user compiled list of equipment and the latency obtained on the LinuxCNC wiki : http://wiki.linuxcnc.org/cgi-bin/-wiki.pl?Latency-Test Please consider adding your info to the list. Also on that page are links to info about fixing some latency problems.

Now we are happy with the latency and must pick a servo period. In most cases a servo period of 1000000 ns is fine (that gives a 1 kHz servo calculation rate - 1000 calculations a second) if you are building a closed loop servo system that controls torque (current) rather then velocity (voltage) a faster rate would be better - something like 200000 (5 kHz calculation rate). The problem with lowering the servo rate is that it leaves less time available for the computer to do other things besides LinuxCNC's calculations. Typically the display (GUI) becomes less responsive. You must decide on a balance. Keep in mind that if you tune your closed loop servo system then change the servo period you probably will need to tune them again.

I/O Control Ports/Boards

PNCconf is capable of configuring machines that have up to two Mesa boards and three parallel ports. Parallel ports can only be used for simple low speed (servo rate) I/O.

Mesa

You must choose at least one Mesa board as PNCconf will not configure the parallel ports to count encoders or output step or PWM signals. The mesa cards available in the selection box are based on what PNCconf finds for firmware on the systems. There are options to add custom firmware and/or *blacklist* (ignore) some firmware or boards using a preference file. If no firmware is found PNCconf will show a warning and use internal sample firmware - no testing will be possible. One point to note is that if you choose two PCI Mesa cards there currently is no way to predict which card is 0 and which is 1 - you must test - moving the cards could change their order. If you configure with two cards both cards must be installed for tests to function.

Parallel Port

Up to 3 parallel ports (referred to as parports) can be used as simple I/O. You must set the address of the parport. You can either enter the Linux parallel port numbering system (0,1,or 2) or enter the actual address. The address for an on board parport is often 0x0278 or 0x0378 (written in hexadecimal) but can be found in the BIOS page. The BIOS page is found when you first start your computer you must press a key to enter it (such as F2). On the BIOS page you can find the parallel port address and set the mode such as SPP, EPP, etc on some computers this info is displayed for a few seconds during start up. For PCI parallel port cards the address can be found by pressing the *parport address search* button. This pops up the help output page with a list of all the PCI devices that can be found. In there should be a reference to a parallel port device with a list of addresses. One of those addresses should work. Not all PCI parallel ports work properly. Either type can be selected as *in* (maximum amount of input pins) or *out* (maximum amount of output pins)

GUI Frontend list

This specifies the graphical display screens LinuxCNC will use. Each one has different option.

AXIS

• fully supports lathes.

- is the most developed and used frontend

- is designed to be used with mouse and keyboard

- is tkinter based so integrates PYVCP (python based virtual control panels) naturally.

- has a 3D graphical window.

- allows VCP integrated on the side or in center tab

TOUCHY

- Touchy was designed to be used with a touchscreen, some minimal physical switches and a MPG wheel.

- requires cycle-start, abort, and single-step signals and buttons

- It also requires shared axis MPG jogging to be selected.

- is GTK based so integrates GLADE VCP (virtual control panels) naturally.

- allows VCP panels integrated in the center Tab

- has no graphical window

- look can be changed with custom themes

MINI

- standard on OEM Sherline machines

- does not use Estop

- no VCP integration

TkLinuxCNC

- hi contrast bright blue screen

- separate graphics window

- no VCP integration

6.3 External Configuration

This page allows you to select external controls such as for jogging or overrides.

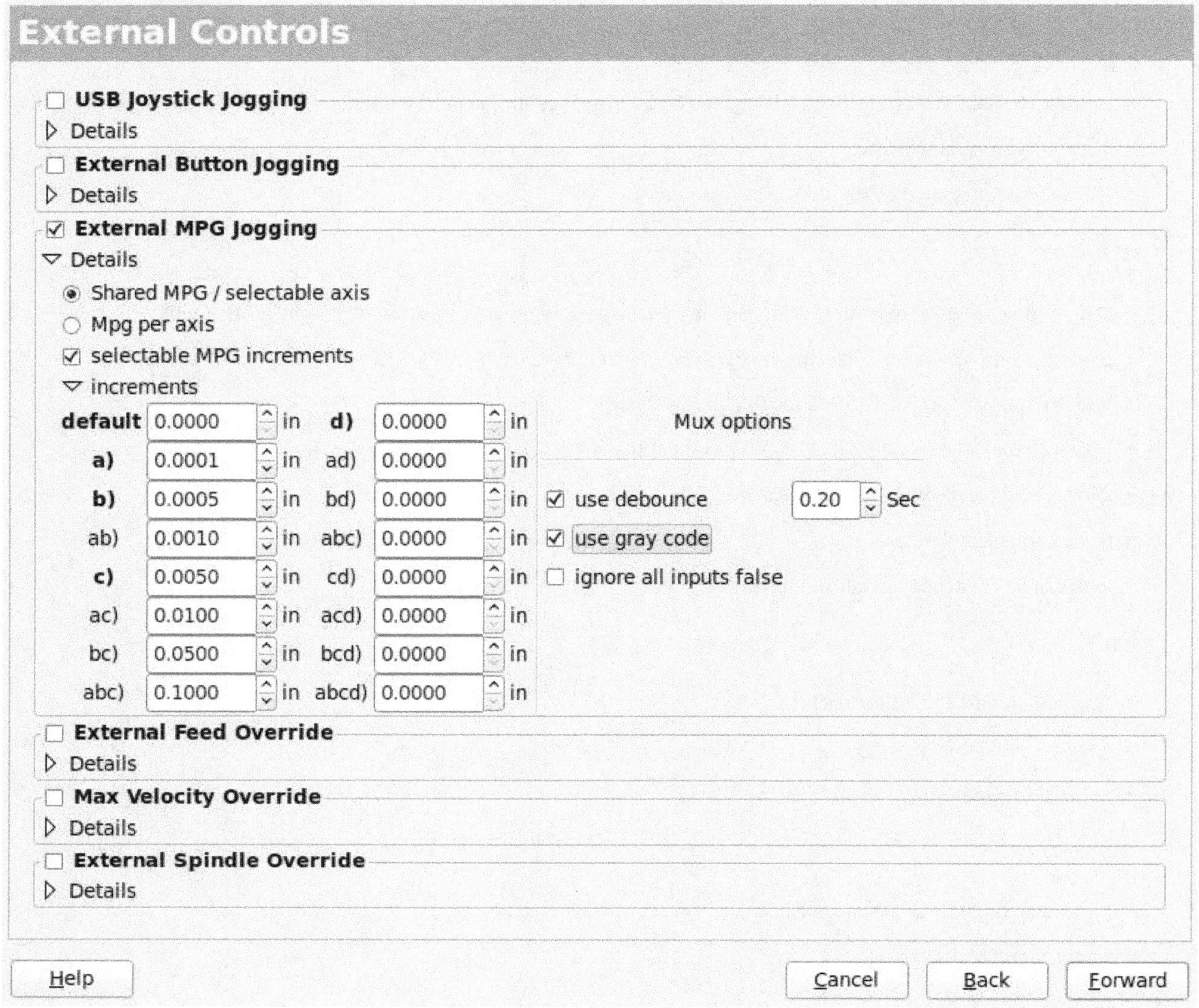

External Controls

☐ **USB Joystick Jogging**
▷ Details

☐ **External Button Jogging**
▷ Details

☑ **External MPG Jogging**
▽ Details
   ⦿ Shared MPG / selectable axis
   ○ Mpg per axis
   ☑ selectable MPG increments
   ▽ increments

						Mux options
default	0.0000 in	**d)**	0.0000 in			
a)	0.0001 in	**ad)**	0.0000 in			
b)	0.0005 in	**bd)**	0.0000 in	☑ use debounce	0.20 Sec	
ab)	0.0010 in	**abc)**	0.0000 in	☑ use gray code		
c)	0.0050 in	**cd)**	0.0000 in	☐ ignore all inputs false		
ac)	0.0100 in	**acd)**	0.0000 in			
bc)	0.0500 in	**bcd)**	0.0000 in			
abc)	0.1000 in	**abcd)**	0.0000 in			

☐ **External Feed Override**
▷ Details

☐ **Max Velocity Override**
▷ Details

☐ **External Spindle Override**
▷ Details

Help   Cancel   Back   Forward

Figure 6.3: GUI External

If you select a Joystick for jogging, You will need it always connected for LinuxCNC to load. To use the analog sticks for useful jogging you probably need to add some custom HAL code. MPG jogging requires a pulse generator connected to a MESA encoder counter. Override controls can either use a pulse generator (MPG) or switches (such as a rotary dial). External buttons might be used with a switch based OEM joystick.

Joystick jogging

Requires a custom *device rule* to be installed in the system. This is a file that LinuxCNC uses to connect to LINUX's device list. PNCconf will help to make this file.

Search for device rule will search the system for rules, you can use this to find the name of devices you have already built with PNCconf.

Add a device rule will allow you to configure a new device by following the prompts. You will need your device available.

test device allows you to load a device, see its pin names and check its functions with halmeter.

joystick jogging uses HALUI and hal_input components.

External buttons

allows jogging the axis with simple buttons at a specified jog rate. Probably best for rapid jogging.

MPG Jogging

Allows you to use a Manual Pulse Generator to jog the machine's axis.

MPG's are often found on commercial grade machines. They output quadrature pulses that can be counted with a MESA encoder counter. PNCconf allows for an MPG per axis or one MPG shared with all axis. It allows for selection of jog speeds using switches or a single speed.

The selectable increments option uses the mux16 component. This component has options such as debounce and gray code to help filter the raw switch input.

Overrides

PNCconf allows overrides of feedrates and/or spindle speed using a pulse generator (MPG) or switches (eg. rotary).

6.4 GUI Configuration

Here you can set defaults for the display screens, add virtual control panels (VCP), and set some LinuxCNC options..

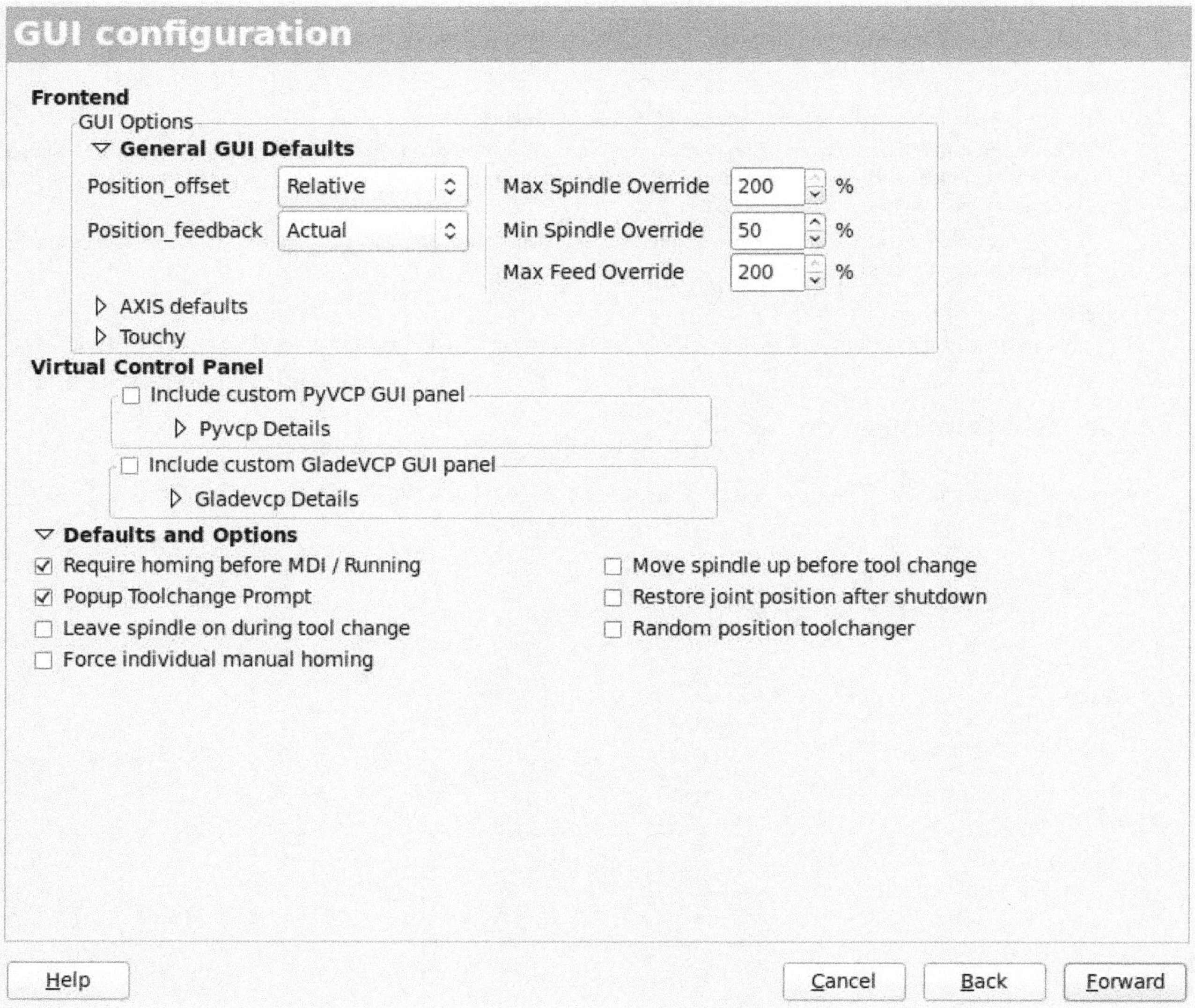

GUI configuration

Frontend

GUI Options

▽ **General GUI Defaults**

Position_offset	Relative ⇕	Max Spindle Override	200 ⌄ %
Position_feedback	Actual ⇕	Min Spindle Override	50 ⌄ %
		Max Feed Override	200 ⌄ %

▷ AXIS defaults
▷ Touchy

Virtual Control Panel

☐ Include custom PyVCP GUI panel

▷ Pyvcp Details

☐ Include custom GladeVCP GUI panel

▷ Gladevcp Details

▽ **Defaults and Options**

☑ Require homing before MDI / Running   ☐ Move spindle up before tool change
☑ Popup Toolchange Prompt   ☐ Restore joint position after shutdown
☐ Leave spindle on during tool change   ☐ Random position toolchanger
☐ Force individual manual homing

Help   Cancel   Back   Forward

Figure 6.4: GUI Configuration

Frontend GUI Options

The default options allows general defaults to be chosen for any display screen.

AXIS defaults are options specific to AXIS. If you choose size , position or force maximize options then PNCconf will ask if it's alright to overwrite a preference file (.axisrc). Unless you have manually added commands to this file it is fine to allow it. Position and force max can be used to move AXIS to a second monitor if the system is capable.

Touchy defaults are options specific to Touchy. Most of Touchy's options can be changed while Touchy is running using the preference page. Touchy uses GTK to draw its screen, and GTK supports themes. Themes controls the basic look and feel of a program. You can download themes from the net or edit them yourself. There are a list of the current themes on the computer that you can pick from. To help some of the text to stand out PNCconf allows you to override the Themes's defaults. The position and force max options can be used to move Touchy to a second monitor if the system is capable.

VCP options

Virtual Control Panels allow one to add custom controls and displays to the screen. AXIS and Touchy can integrate these controls inside the screen in designated positions. There are two kinds of VCPs - pyVCP which uses *Tkinter* to draw the screen and GLADE VCP that uses *GTK* to draw the screen.

PyVCP

PyVCPs screen XML file can only be hand built. PyVCPs fit naturally in with AXIS as they both use TKinter.

HAL pins are created for the user to connect to inside their custom HAL file. There is a sample spindle display panel for the user to use as-is or build on. You may select a blank file that you can later add your controls *widgets* to or select a spindle display sample that will display spindle speed and indicate if the spindle is at requested speed.

PNCconf will connect the proper spindle display HAL pins for you. If you are using AXIS then the panel will be integrated on the right side. If not using AXIS then the panel will be separate *stand-alone* from the frontend screen.

You can use the geometry options to size and move the panel, for instance to move it to a second screen if the system is capable. If you press the *Display sample panel* button the size and placement options will be honoured.

GLADE VCP

GLADE VCPs fit naturally inside of TOUCHY screen as they both use GTK to draw them, but by changing GLADE VCP's theme it can be made to blend pretty well in AXIS. (try Redmond)

It uses a graphical editor to build its XML files. HAL pins are created for the user to connect to, inside of their custom HAL file.

GLADE VCP also allows much more sophisticated (and complicated) programming interaction, which PNCconf currently doesn't leverage. (see GLADE VCP in the manual)

PNCconf has sample panels for the user to use as-is or build on. With GLADE VCP PNCconf will allow you to select different options on your sample display.

Under *sample options* select which ones you would like. The zero buttons use HALUI commands which you could edit later in the HALUI section.

Auto Z touch-off also requires the classicladder touch-off program and a probe input selected. It requires a conductive touch-off plate and a grounded conductive tool. For an idea on how it works see:

http://wiki.linuxcnc.org/cgi-bin/wiki.pl?ClassicLadderExamples#Single_button_probe_touchoff

Under *Display Options*, size, position, and force max can be used on a *stand-alone* panel for such things as placing the screen on a second monitor if the system is capable.

You can select a GTK theme which sets the basic look and feel of the panel. You Usually want this to match the frontend screen. These options will be used if you press the *Display sample button*. With GLADE VCP depending on the frontend screen, you can select where the panel will display.

You can force it to be stand-alone or with AXIS it can be in the center or on the right side, with Touchy it can be in the center.

Defaults and Options

- Require homing before MDI / Running
  - If you want to be able to move the machine before homing uncheck this checkbox.
- Popup Tool Prompt
  - Choose between an on screen prompt for tool changes or export standard signal names for a User supplied custom tool changer Hal file
- Leave spindle on during tool change:
  - Used for lathes
- Force individual manual homing
- Move spindle up before tool change
- Restore joint position after shutdown
  - Used for non-trivial kinematics machines
- Random position toolchangers
  - Used for toolchangers that do not return the tool to the same pocket. You will need to add custom HAL code to support toolchangers.

6.5   Mesa Configuration

The Mesa configuration pages allow one to utilize different firmwares. On the basic page you selected a Mesa card here you pick the available firmware and select what and how many components are available.

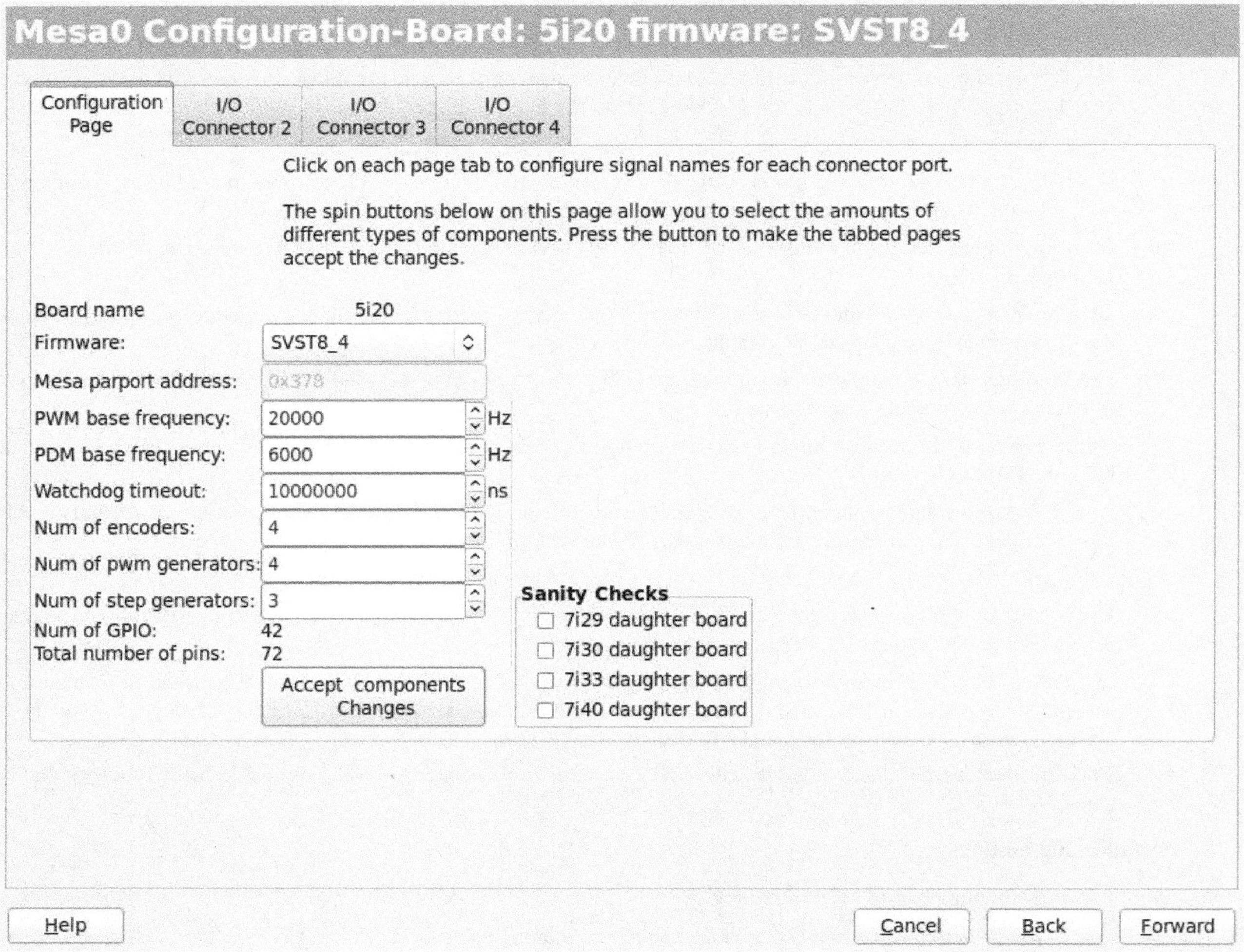

Figure 6.5: Mesa Configuration

Parport address is used only with Mesa parport card, the 7i43. An onboard parallel port usually uses 0x278 or 0x378 though you should be able to find the address from the BIOS page. The 7i43 requires the parallel port to use the EPP mode, again set in the BIOS page. If using a PCI parallel port the address can be searched for by using the search button on the basic page.

Note

Many PCI cards do not support the EPP protocol properly.

PDM PWM and 3PWM base frequency sets the balance between ripple and linearity. If using Mesa daughter boards the docs for the board should give recommendations

Important

It's important to follow these to avoid damage and get the best performance.

```
The 7i33 requires PDM and a PDM base frequency of 6 mHz
The 7i29 requires PWM and a PWM base frequency of 20 Khz
The 7i30 requires PWM and a PWM base frequency of 20 Khz
The 7i40 requires PWM and a PWM base frequency of 50 Khz
The 7i48 requires UDM and a PWM base frequency of 24 Khz
```

Watchdog time out is used to set how long the MESA board will wait before killing outputs if communication is interrupted from the computer. Please remember Mesa uses *active low* outputs meaning that when the output pin is on, it is low (approx 0 volts) and if it's off the output in high (approx 5 volts) make sure your equipment is safe when in the off (watchdog bitten) state.

You may choose the number of available components by deselecting unused ones. Not all component types are available with all firmware.

Choosing less then the maximum number of components allows one to gain more GPIO pins. If using daughter boards keep in mind you must not deselect pins that the card uses. For instance some firmware supports two 7i33 cards, If you only have one you may deselect enough components to utilize the connector that supported the second 7i33. Components are deselected numerically by the highest number first then down with out skipping a number. If by doing this the components are not where you want them then you must use a different firmware. The firmware dictates where, what and the max amounts of the components. Custom firmware is possible, ask nicely when contacting the LinuxCNC developers and Mesa. Using custom firmware in PNCconf requires special procedures and is not always possible - Though I try to make PNCconf as flexible as possible.

After choosing all these options press the *Accept Component Changes* button and PNCconf will update the I/O setup pages. Only I/O tabs will be shown for available connectors, depending on the Mesa board.

6.6 Mesa I/O Setup

The tabs are used to configure the input and output pins of the Mesa boards. PNCconf allows one to create custom signal names for use in custom HAL files.

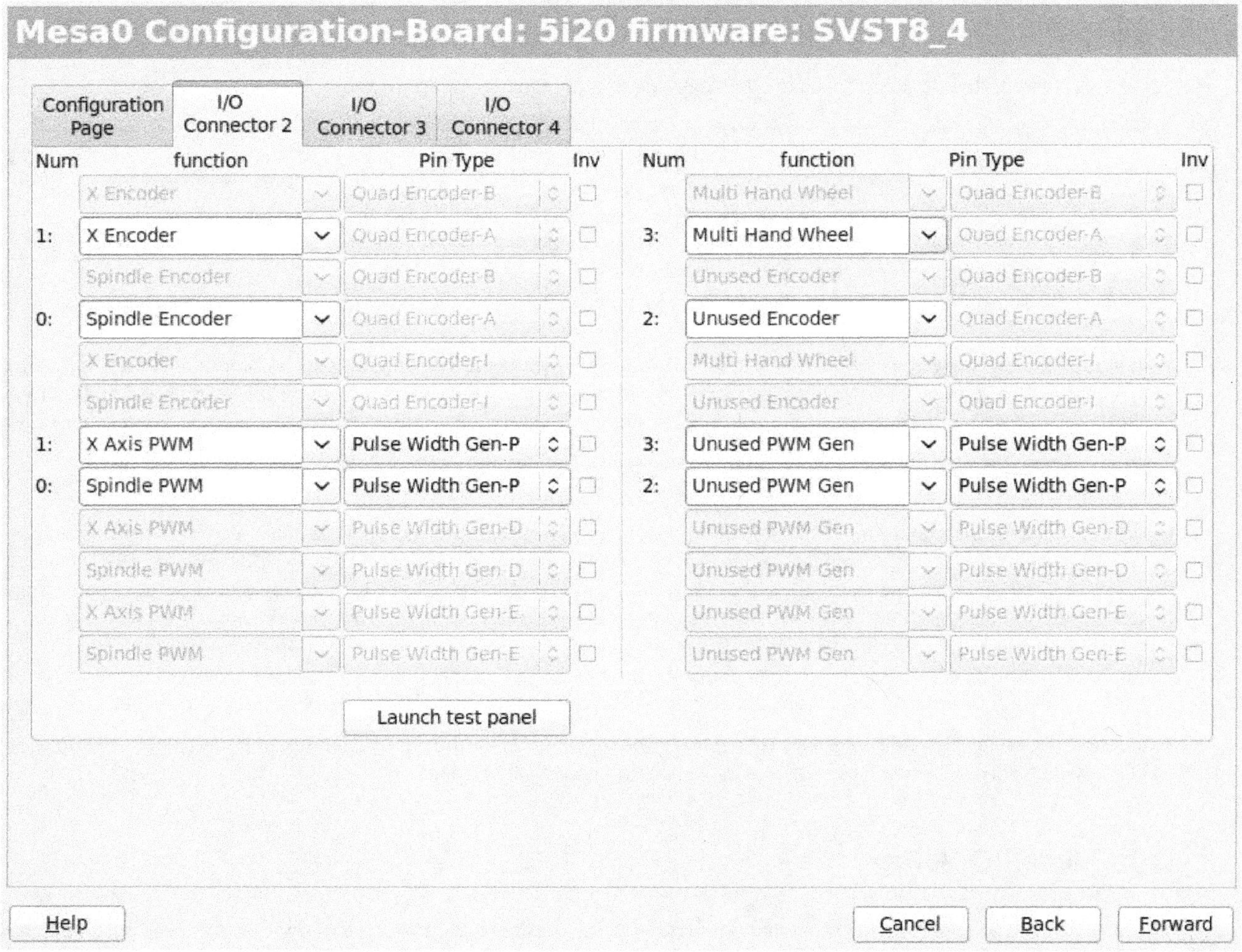

Figure 6.6: Mesa I/O C2

On this tab with this firmware the components are setup for a 7i33 daughter board, usually used with closed loop servos. Note the component numbers of the encoder counters and PWM drivers are not in numerical order. This follows the daughter board requirements.

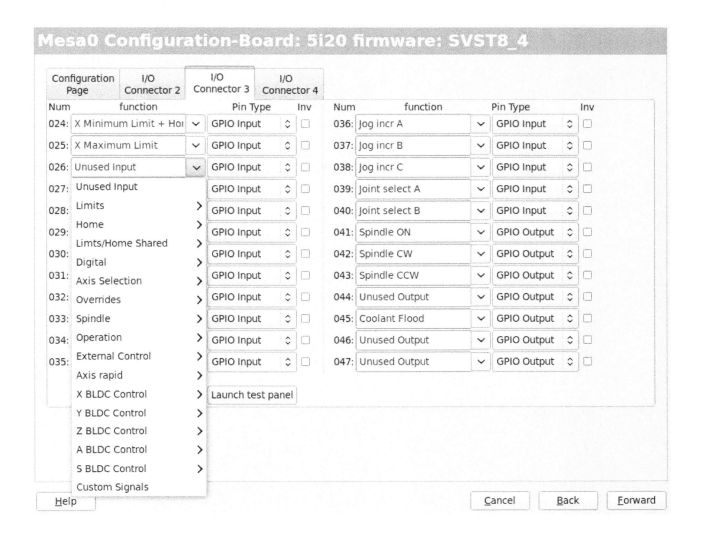

Figure 6.7: Mesa I/O C3

On this tab all the pins are GPIO. Note the 3 digit numbers - they will match the HAL pin number. GPIO pins can be selected as input or output and can be inverted.

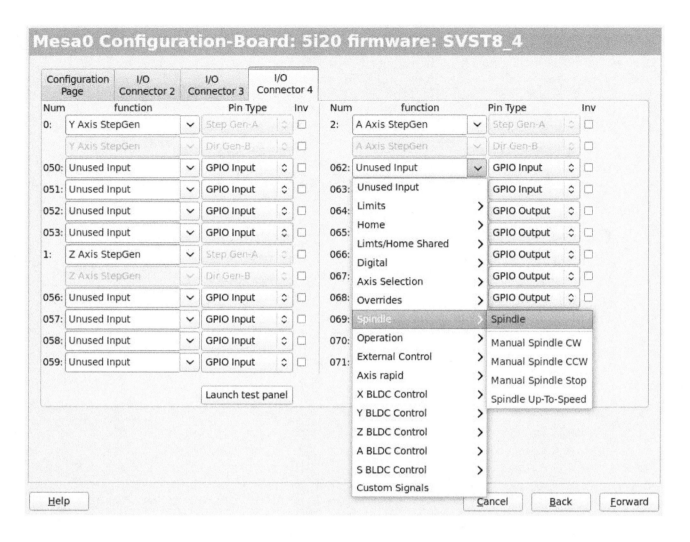

Figure 6.8: Mesa I/O C4

On this tab there are a mix of step generators and GPIO. Step generators output and direction pins can be inverted. Note that inverting a Step Gen-A pin (the step output pin) changes the step timing. It should match what your controller expects.

6.7 Parport configuration

First Parallel Port set for OUTPUT

Outputs (PC to Machine):		Invert	Inputs (Machine to PC):		Invert
Pin 1:	Digital out 0	☐	Pin 2:	Unused Input	☐
Pin 2:	Machine Is Enabled	☐	Pin 3:	Unused Input	☐
Pin 3:	X Amplifier Enable	☐	Pin 4:	Unused Input	☐
Pin 4:	Z Amplifier Enable	☐	Pin 5:	Unused Input	☐
Pin 5:	Unused Output	☐	Pin 6:	Unused Input	☐
Pin 6:	Unused Output	☐	Pin 7:	Unused Input	☐
Pin 7:	Unused Output	☐	Pin 8:	Unused Input	☐
Pin 8:	Unused Output	☐	Pin 9:	Unused Input	☐
Pin 9:	Unused Output	☐	Pin 10:	Digital in 0	☐
Pin 14:	Unused Output	☐	Pin 11:	Unused Input	☐
Pin 16:	Unused Output	☐	Pin 12:	Unused Input	☐
Pin 17:	Unused Output	☐	Pin 13:	Unused Input	☐
			Pin 15:	Unused Input	☐

Launch Test Panel

Help   Cancel   Back   Forward

The parallel port can be used for simple I/O similar to Mesa's GPIO pins.

6.8   Axis Configuration

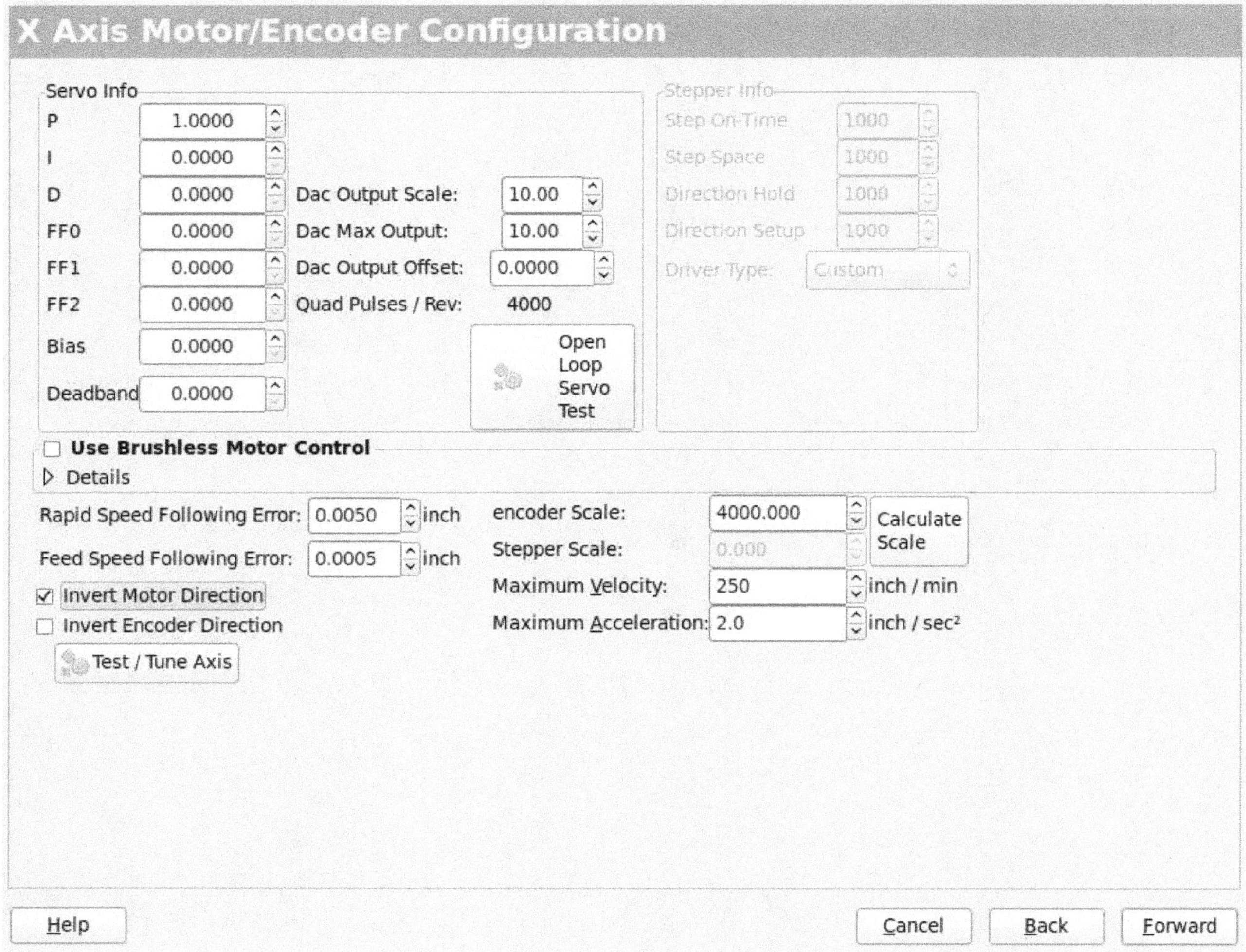

Figure 6.9: Axis Drive Configuration

This page allows configuring and testing of the motor and/or encoder combination . If using a servo motor an open loop test is available, if using a stepper a tuning test is available.

Open Loop Test

An open loop test is important as it confirms the direction of the motor and encoder. The motor should move the axis in the positive direction when the positive button is pushed and also the encoder should count in the postie direction. The axis movement should follow the Machinery's Handbook [1] standards or AXIS graphical display will not make much sense. Hopefully the help page and diagrams can help figure this out. Note that axis directions are based on TOOL movement not table movement. There is no acceleration ramping with the open loop test so start with lower DAC numbers. By moving the axis a known distance one can confirm the encoder scaling. The encoder should count even without the amp enabled depending on how power is supplied to the encoder.

---

[1] "axis nomenclature" in the chapter "Numerical Control" in the "Machinery's Handbook" published by Industrial Press.

Warning

If the motor and encoder do not agree on counting direction then the servo will run away when using PID control.

Since at the moment PID settings can not be tested in PNCconf the settings are really for when you re-edit a config - enter your tested PID settings.

DAC scaling, max output and offset are used to tailor the DAC output.

Compute DAC

These two values are the scale and offset factors for the axis output to the motor amplifiers. The second value (offset) is subtracted from the computed output (in volts), and divided by the first value (scale factor), before being written to the D/A converters. The units on the scale value are in true volts per DAC output volts. The units on the offset value are in volts. These can be used to linearize a DAC.

Specifically, when writing outputs, the LinuxCNC first converts the desired output in quasi-SI units to raw actuator values, e.g., volts for an amplifier DAC. This scaling looks like: The value for scale can be obtained analytically by doing a unit analysis, i.e., units are [output SI units]/[actuator units]. For example, on a machine with a velocity mode amplifier such that 1 volt results in 250 mm/sec velocity, Note that the units of the offset are in machine units, e.g., mm/sec, and they are pre-subtracted from the sensor readings. The value for this offset is obtained by finding the value of your output which yields 0.0 for the actuator output. If the DAC is linearized, this offset is normally 0.0.

The scale and offset can be used to linearize the DAC as well, resulting in values that reflect the combined effects of amplifier gain, DAC non-linearity, DAC units, etc. To do this, follow this procedure:

- Build a calibration table for the output, driving the DAC with a desired voltage and measuring the result:

Table 6.1: Output Voltage Measurements

Raw	Measured
-10	**-9.93**
-9	**-8.83**
0	**-0.96**
1	**-0.03**
9	**9.87**
10	**10.07**

- Do a least-squares linear fit to get coefficients a, b such that meas=a*raw+b

- Note that we want raw output such that our measured result is identical to the commanded output. This means

  - cmd=a*raw+b

  - raw=(cmd-b)/a

- As a result, the a and b coefficients from the linear fit can be used as the scale and offset for the controller directly.

MAX OUTPUT: The maximum value for the output of the PID compensation that is written to the motor amplifier, in volts. The computed output value is clamped to this limit. The limit is applied before scaling to raw output units. The value is applied symmetrically to both the plus and the minus side.

Tuning Test The tuning test unfortunately only works with stepper based systems. Again confirm the directions on the axis is correct. Then test the system by running the axis back and forth, If the acceleration or max speed is too high you will lose steps. While jogging, Keep in mind it can take a while for an axis with low acceleration to stop. Limit switches are not functional during this test. You can set a pause time so each end of the test movement. This would allow you to set up and read a dial indicator to see if you are loosing steps.

Stepper Timing Stepper timing needs to be tailored to the step controller's requirements. Pncconf supplies some default controller timing or allows custom timing settings . See http://wiki.linuxcnc.org/cgi-bin/wiki.pl?Stepper_Drive_Timing for some more known timing numbers (feel free to add ones you have figured out). If in doubt use large numbers such as 5000 this will only limit max speed.

Brushless Motor Control These options are used to allow low level control of brushless motors using special firmware and daughter boards. It also allows conversion of HALL sensors from one manufacturer to another. It is only partially supported and will require one to finish the HAL connections. Contact the mail-list or forum for more help.

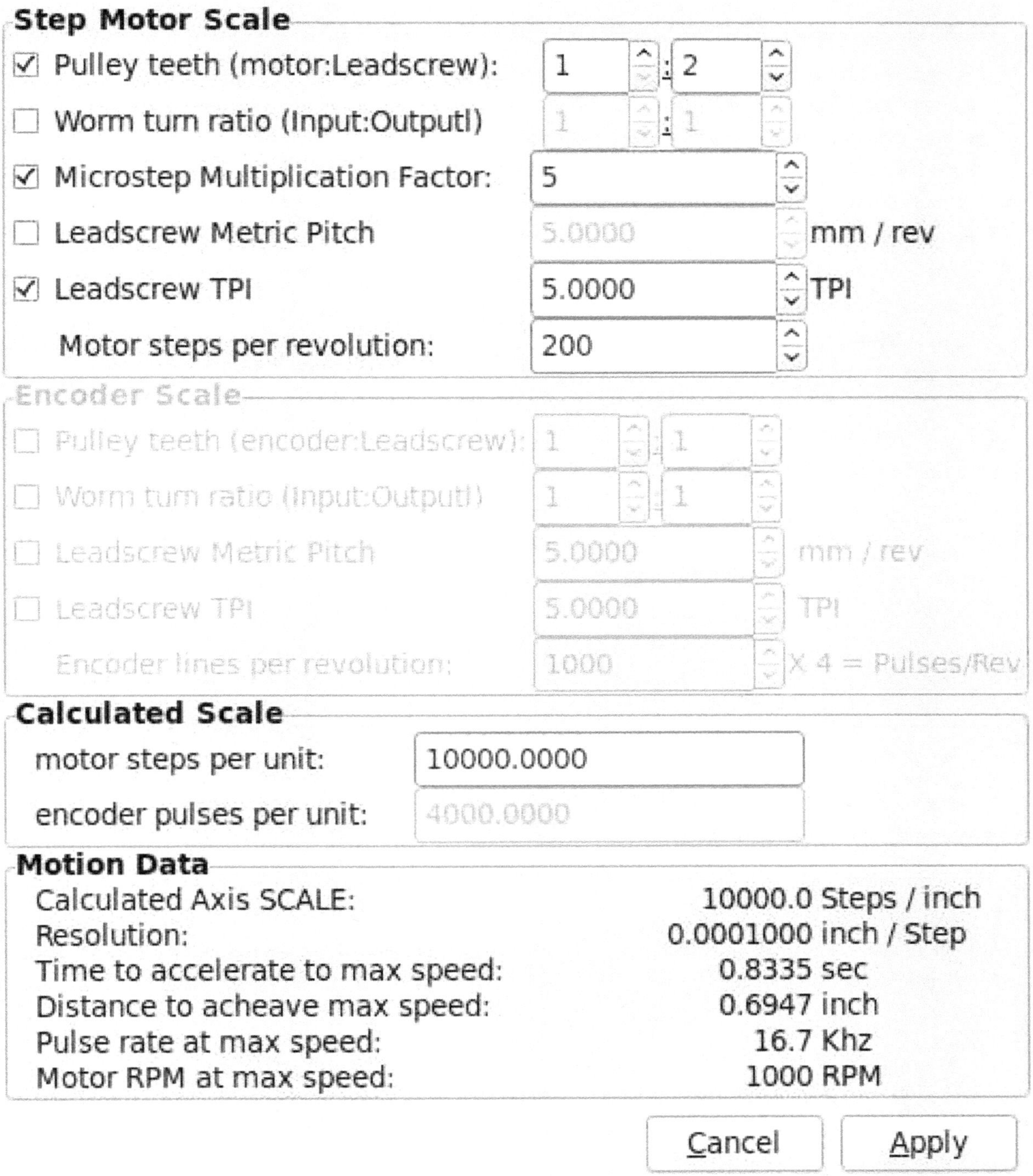

Step Motor Scale

☑ Pulley teeth (motor:Leadscrew): `1` `:` `2`

☐ Worm turn ratio (Input:Outputl) `1` `:` `1`

☑ Microstep Multiplication Factor: `5`

☐ Leadscrew Metric Pitch `5.0000` mm / rev

☑ Leadscrew TPI `5.0000` TPI

   Motor steps per revolution: `200`

Encoder Scale

☐ Pulley teeth (encoder:Leadscrew): `1` `1`

☐ Worm turn ratio (Input:Outputl) `1` `1`

☐ Leadscrew Metric Pitch `5.0000` mm / rev

☐ Leadscrew TPI `5.0000` TPI

   Encoder lines per revolution: `1000` X 4 = Pulses/Rev

Calculated Scale

   motor steps per unit: `10000.0000`

   encoder pulses per unit: `4000.0000`

Motion Data

Calculated Axis SCALE:	10000.0 Steps / inch
Resolution:	0.0001000 inch / Step
Time to accelerate to max speed:	0.8335 sec
Distance to acheave max speed:	0.6947 inch
Pulse rate at max speed:	16.7 Khz
Motor RPM at max speed:	1000 RPM

Cancel   Apply

Figure 6.10: Axis Scale Calculation

The scale settings can be directly entered or one can use the *calculate scale* button to assist. Use the check boxes to select appropriate calculations. Note that *pulley teeth* requires the number of teeth not the gear ratio. Worm turn ratio is just the opposite it requires the gear ratio. If your happy with the scale press apply otherwise push cancel and enter the scale directly.

X Axis Configuration

Positive Travel Distance (Machine zero Origin to end of + travel):		8.0
Negative Travel Distance (Machine zero Origin to end of - travel):		0.0
Home Position location (offset from machine zero Origin):		0.0
Home Switch location (Offset from machine zero Origin):		0.0

Home Search Velocity: `3`   inch / min

Home Search Direction: `Towards Negative limit  ◇`

Home latch Velocity: `1`   inch / min

Home Latch Direction: `Same  ◇`

Home Final Velocity: `0`   inch / min

Use Encoder Index For Home: `NO  ◇`

☐ Use Compensation File: `Type 1  ◇`   filename: `xcompensation`

☐ Use Backlash Compensation: `0.0000  ◇`

Help		Cancel	Back	Forward

Figure 6.11: Axis Configuration

Also refer to the diagram tab for two examples of home and limit switches. These are two examples of many different ways to set homing and limits.

Important
It is very important to start with the axis moving in the right direction or else getting homing right is very difficult!

Remember positive and negative directions refer to the TOOL not the table as per the Machinists handbook.

ON A TYPICAL KNEE OR BED MILL

- when the TABLE moves out that is the positive Y direction

- when the TABLE moves left that is the positive X direction

- when the TABLE moves down that is the positive Z direction

- when the HEAD moves up that is the positive Z direction

ON A TYPICAL LATHE

- when the TOOL moves right, away from the chuck

- that is the positive Z direction

- when the TOOL moves toward the operator

- that is the positive X direction. Some lathes have X

- opposite (eg tool on back side), that will work fine but

- AXIS graphical display can not be made to reflect this.

When using homing and / or limit switches LinuxCNC expects the HAL signals to be true when the switch is being pressed / tripped. If the signal is wrong for a limit switch then LinuxCNC will think the machine is on end of limit all the time. If the home switch search logic is wrong LinuxCNC will seem to home in the wrong direction. What it actually is doing is trying to BACK off the home switch.

Decide on limit switch location.

Limit switches are the back up for software limits in case something electrical goes wrong eg. servo runaway. Limit switches should be placed so that the machine does not hit the physical end of the axis movement. Remember the axis will coast past the contact point if moving fast. Limit switches should be *active low* on the machine. eg. power runs through the switches all the time - a loss of power (open switch) trips. While one could wire them the other way, this is fail safe. This may need to be inverted so that the HAL signal in LinuxCNC in *active high* - a TRUE means the switch was tripped. When starting LinuxCNC if you get an on-limit warning, and axis is NOT tripping the switch, inverting the signal is probably the solution. (use HALMETER to check the corresponding HAL signal eg. axis.0.pos-lim-sw-in X axis positive limit switch)

Decide on the home switch location.

If you are using limit switches You may as well use one as a home switch. A separate home switch is useful if you have a long axis that in use is usually a long way from the limit switches or moving the axis to the ends presents problems of interference with material. eg a long shaft in a lathe makes it hard to home to limits with out the tool hitting the shaft, so a separate home switch closer to the middle may be better. If you have an encoder with index then the home switch acts as a course home and the index will be the actual home location.

Decide on the MACHINE ORIGIN position.

MACHINE ORIGIN is what LinuxCNC uses to reference all user coordinate systems from. I can think of little reason it would need to be in any particular spot. There are only a few G codes that can access the MACHINE COORDINATE system.(G53, G30 and G28) If using tool-change-at-G30 option having the Origin at the tool change position may be convenient. By convention, it may be easiest to have the ORIGIN at the home switch.

Decide on the (final) HOME POSITION.

this just places the carriage at a consistent and convenient position after LinuxCNC figures out where the ORIGIN is.

Measure / calculate the positive / negative axis travel distances.

Move the axis to the origin. Mark a reference on the movable slide and the non-moveable support (so they are in line) move the machine to the end of limits. Measure between the marks that is one of the travel distances. Move the table to the other end of travel. Measure the marks again. That is the other travel distance. If the ORIGIN is at one of the limits then that travel distance will be zero.

(machine) ORIGIN
> The Origin is the MACHINE zero point. (not the zero point you set your cutter / material at). LinuxCNC uses this point to reference everything else from. It should be inside the software limits. LinuxCNC uses the home switch location to calculate the origin position (when using home switches or must be manually set if not using home switches.

Travel distance
> This is the maximum distance the axis can travel in each direction. This may or may not be able to be measured directly from origin to limit switch. The positive and negative travel distances should add up to the total travel distance.

POSITIVE TRAVEL DISTANCE

    This is the distance the Axis travels from the Origin to the positive travel distance or the total travel minus the negative travel distance. You would set this to zero if the origin is positioned at the positive limit. The will always be zero or a positive number.

NEGATIVE TRAVEL DISTANCE

    This is the distance the Axis travels from the Origin to the negative travel distance. or the total travel minus the positive travel distance. You would set this to zero if the origin is positioned at the negative limit. This will always be zero or a negative number. If you forget to make this negative PNCconf will do it internally.

(Final) HOME POSITION

    This is the position the home sequence will finish at. It is referenced from the Origin so can be negative or positive depending on what side of the Origin it is located. When at the (final) home position if you must move in the Positive direction to get to the Origin, then the number will be negative.

HOME SWITCH LOCATION

    This is the distance from the home switch to the Origin. It could be negative or positive depending on what side of the Origin it is located. When at the home switch location if you must move in the Positive direction to get to the Origin, then the number will be negative. If you set this to zero then the Origin will be at the location of the limit switch (plus distance to find index if used)

Home Search Velocity

    Course home search velocity in units per minute.

Home Search Direction

    Sets the home switch search direction either negative (ie. towards negative limit switch) or positive (ie. towards positive limit switch)

Home Latch Velocity

    Fine Home search velocity in units per minute

Home Final Velocity

    Velocity used from latch position to (final) home position in units per minute. Set to 0 for max rapid speed

Home latch Direction

    Allows setting of the latch direction to the same or opposite of the search direction.

Use Encoder Index For Home

    LinuxCNC will search for an encoder index pulse while in the latch stage of homing.

Use Compensation File

    Allows specifying a Comp filename and type. Allows sophisticated compensation. See Manual.

Use Backlash Compensation

    Allows setting of simple backlash compensation. Can not be used with Compensation File. See Manual.

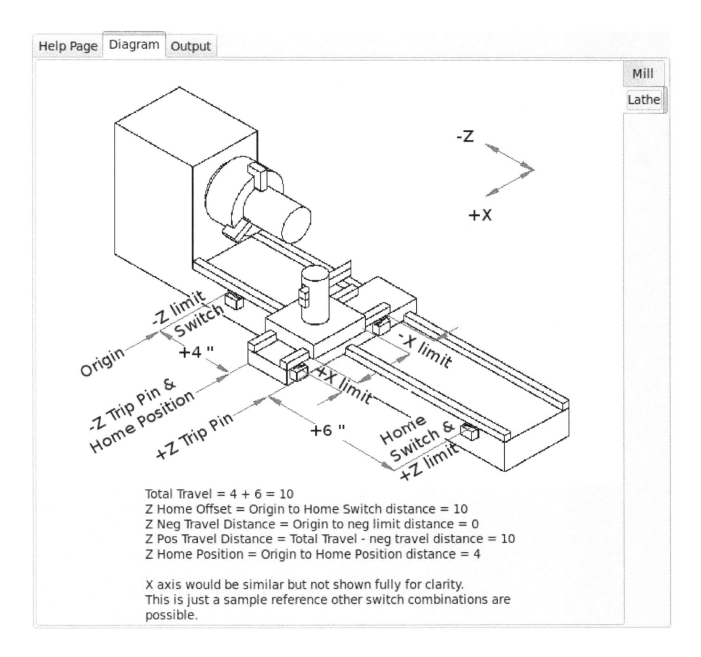

Figure 6.12: AXIS Help Diagram

The diagrams should help to demonstrate an example of limit switches and standard axis movement directions. In this example the Z axis was two limit switches, the positive switch is shared as a home switch. The MACHINE ORIGIN (zero point) is located at the negative limit. The left edge of the carriage is the negative trip pin and the right the positive trip pin. We wish the FINAL HOME POSITION to be 4 inches away from the ORIGIN on the positive side. If the carriage was moved to the positive limit we would measure 10 inches between the negative limit and the negative trip pin.

6.9   Spindle Configuration

If you select spindle signals then this page is available to configure spindle control.

Tip

Many of the option on this page will not show unless the proper option was selected on previous pages!

Figure 6.13: Spindle Configuration

This page is similar to the axis motor configuration page.

There are some differences:

- Unless one has chosen a stepper driven spindle there is no acceleration or velocity limiting.

- There is no support for gear changes or ranges.

- If you picked a VCP spindle display option then spindle-at-speed scale and filter settings may be shown.

- Spindle-at-speed allows LinuxCNC to wait till the spindle is at the requested speed before moving the axis. This is particularly handy on lathes with constant surface feed and large speed diameter changes. It requires either encoder feedback or a digital spindle-at-speed signal typically connected to a VFD drive.

- If using encoder feedback, you may select a spindle-at-speed scale setting that specifies how close the actual speed must be to the requested speed to be considered at-speed.

- If using encoder feedback, the VCP speed display can be erratic - the filter setting can be used to smooth out the display. The encoder scale must be set for the encoder count / gearing used.

- If you are using a single input for a spindle encoder you must add the line: setp hm2_7i43.0.encoder.00.counter-mode 1 (changing the board name and encoder number to your requirements) into a custom HAL file. See the Hostmot2 section on encoders for more info about counter mode.

6.10 Advanced Options

This allows setting of HALUI commands and loading of classicladder and sample ladder programs. If you selected GLADE VCP options such as for zeroing axis, there will be commands showing. See the manual about info on HALUI for using custom halcmds. There are several ladder program options. The Estop program allows an external ESTOP switch or the GUI frontend to throw an Estop. It also has a timed lube pump signal. The Z auto touch-off is with a touch-off plate, the GLADE VCP touch-off button and special HALUI commands to set the current user origin to zero and rapid clear. The serial modbus program is basically a blank template program that sets up classicladder for serial modbus. See the classicladder section in the manual.

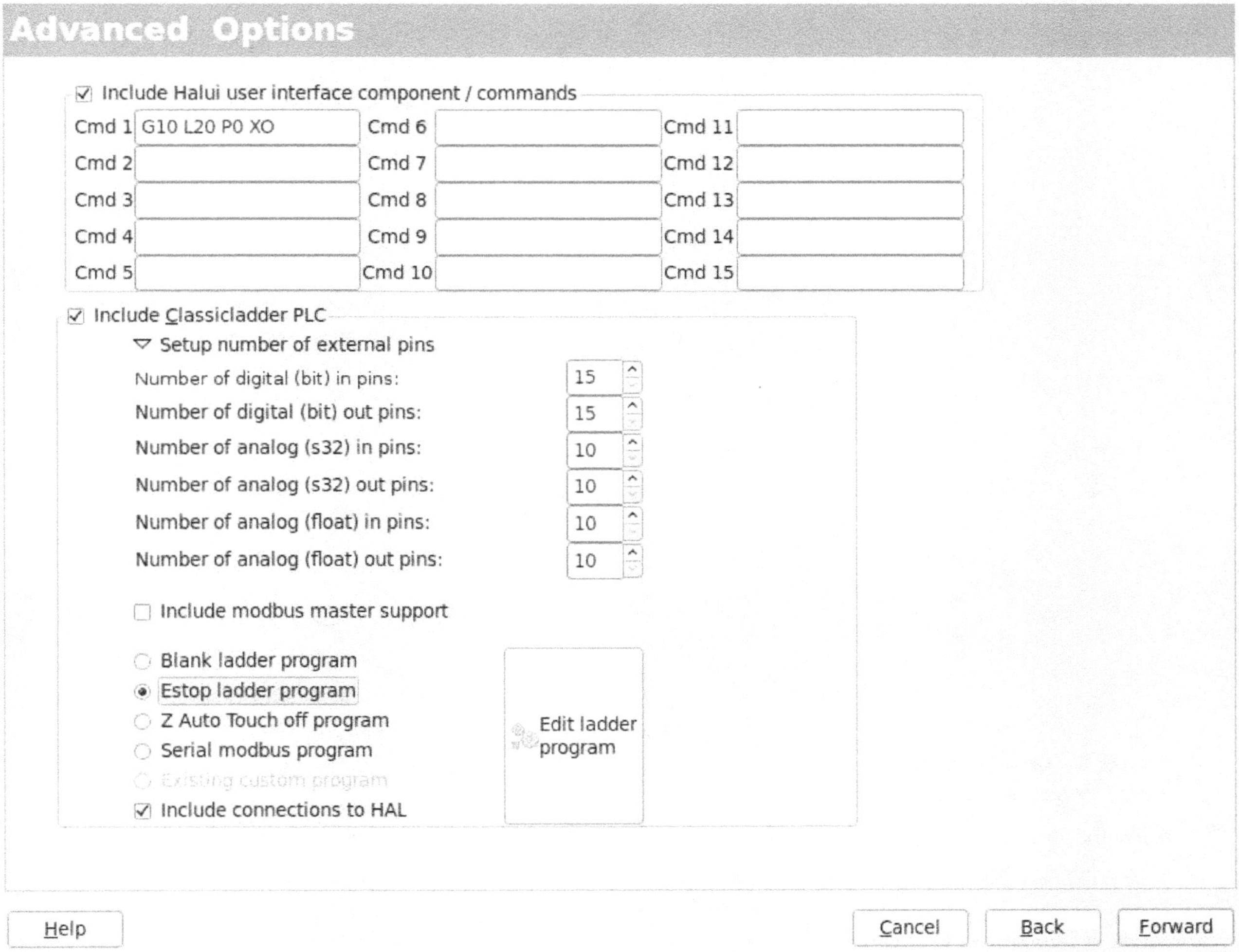

Figure 6.14: Advanced Options

6.11 HAL Components

On this page you can add additional HAL components you might need for custom HAL files. In this way one should not have to hand edit the main HAL file, while still allowing user needed components.

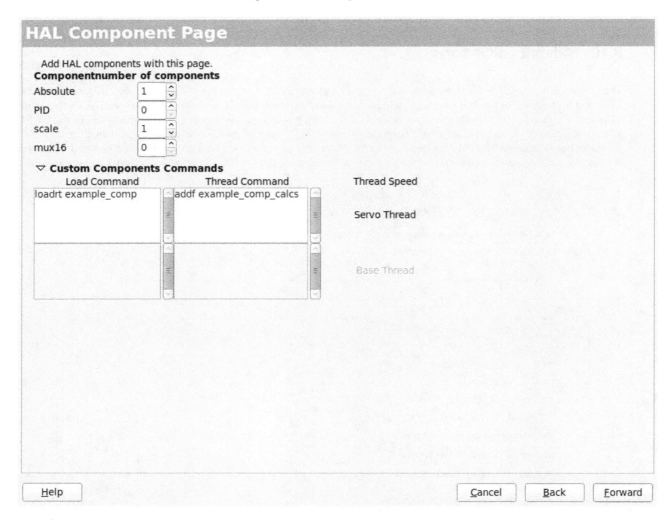

Figure 6.15: HAL Components

The first selection is components that pncconf uses internally. You may configure pncconf to load extra instances of the components for your custom HAL file.

Select the number of instances your custom file will need, pncconf will add what it needs after them.

Meaning if you need 2 and pncconf needs 1 pncconf will load 3 instances and use the last one.

Custom Component Commands
This selection will allow you to load HAL components that pncconf does not use. Add the loadrt or loadusr command, under the heading *loading command* Add the addf command under the heading *Thread command*. The components will be added to the thread between reading of inputs and writing of outputs, in the order you write them in the *thread command*.

6.12   Advanced Usage Of PNCconf

PNCconf does its best to allow flexible customization by the user. PNCconf has support for custom signal names, custom loading of components, custom HAL files and custom firmware.

There are also signal names that PNCconf always provides regardless of options selected, for user's custom HAL files With some thought most customizations should work regardless if you later select different options in PNCconf.

Eventually if the customizations are beyond the scope of PNCconf's frame work you can use PNCconf to build a base config or use one of LinuxCNC's sample configurations and just hand edit it to what ever you want.

Custom Signal Names

    If you wish to connect a component to something in a custom HAL file write a unique signal name in the combo entry box. Certain components will add endings to your custom signal name:

Encoders will add < customname > +:

- position
- count
- velocity
- index-enable
- reset

Steppers add:

- enable
- counts
- position-cmd
- position-fb
- velocity-fb

PWM add:

- enable
- value

GPIO pins will just have the entered signal name connected to it

In this way one can connect to these signals in the custom HAL files and still have the option to move them around later.

Custom Signal Names

    The Hal Components page can be used to load components needed by a user for customization.

Loading Custom Firmware

    PNCconf searches for firmware on the system and then looks for the XML file that it can convert to what it understands. These XML files are only supplied for officially released firmware from the LinuxCNC team. To utilize custom firmware one must convert it to an array that PNCconf understands and add its filepath to PNCconf's preference file. By default this path searches the desktop for a folder named custom_firmware and a file named firmware.py.

The hidden preference file is in the user's home file, is named .pncconf-preferences and require one to select *show hidden files* to see and edit it. The contents of this file can be seen when you first load PNCconf - press the help button and look at the output page.

Ask on the LinuxCNC mail-list or forum for info about converting custom firmware. Not all firmware can be utilized with PNCconf.

Custom HAL Files

There are four custom files that you can use to add HAL commands to:

- custom.hal is for HAL commands that don't have to be run after the GUI frontend loads. It is run after the configuration-named HAL file.

- custom_postgui.hal is for commands that must be run after AXIS loads or a standalone PYVCP display loads.

- custom_gvcp.hal is for commands that must be run after glade VCP is loaded.

- shutdown.hal is for commands to run when LinuxCNC shuts down in a controlled manner.

Chapter 7

Running LinuxCNC

7.1 Invoking LinuxCNC

After installation, LinuxCNC starts just like any other Linux program: run it from the terminal by issuing the command *emc*, or select it in the Applications - CNC menu.

7.2 Configuration Selector

By default, the Configuration Selector dialog is shown when you first run LinuxCNC. Your own personalized configurations are shown at the top of the list, followed by sample configurations. Because each sample configuration is for a different type of hardware interface, almost all will not run without the hardware installed. The configurations listed under the category *sim* run entirely without attached hardware.

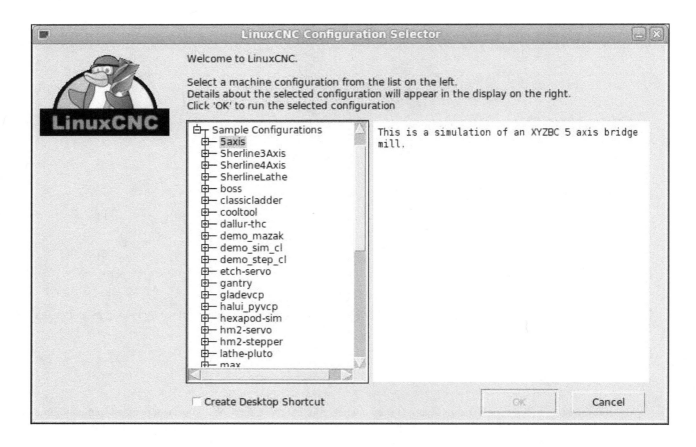

Figure 7.1: LinuxCNC Configuration Selector

Click any of the listed configurations to display specific information about it. Double-click a configuration or click OK to start the configuration. Select *Create Desktop Shortcut* and then click OK to add an icon on the Ubuntu desktop to directly launch this configuration without showing the Configuration Selector screen.

When you select a configuration from the Sample Configurations section, it will automaticly place a copy of that config in the emc/configs directory.

7.3 Next steps in configuration

After finding the sample configuration that uses the same interface hardware as your machine, and saving a copy to your home directory, you can customize it according to the details of your machine. Refer to the Integrator Manual for topics on configuration.

Chapter 8

Linux FAQ

These are some basic Linux commands and techniques for new to Linux users. More complete information can be found on the web or by using the man pages.

8.1 Automatic Login

When you install LinuxCNC with the Ubuntu LiveCD the default is to have to log in each time you turn the computer on. To enable automatic login go to *System > Administration > Login Window*. If it is a fresh install the Login Window might take a second or three to pop up. You will have to have your password that you used for the install to gain access to the Login Window Preferences window. In the Security tab check off Enable Automatic Login and pick a user name from the list (that would be you).

8.2 Automatic Startup

To have LinuxCNC start automatically with your config after turning on the computer go to *System > Preferences > Sessions > Startup Applications*, click Add. Browse to your config and select the .ini file. When the file picker dialog closes, add emc and a space in front of the path to your .ini file.

Example:

```
emc /home/mill/emc2/config/mill/mill.ini
```

8.3 Man Pages

Man pages are automatically generated manual pages in most cases. Man pages are usually available for most programs and commands in Linux.

To view a man page open up a terminal window by going to *Applications > Accessories > Terminal*. For example if you wanted to find out something about the find command in the terminal window type:

```
man find
```

Use the Page Up and Page Down keys to view the man page and the Q key to quit viewing.

8.4   List Modules

Sometimes when troubleshooting you need to get a list of modules that are loaded. In a terminal window type:

```
lsmod
```

If you want to send the output from lsmod to a text file in a terminal window type:

```
lsmod > mymod.txt
```

The resulting text file will be located in the home directory if you did not change directories when you opened up the terminal window and it will be named mymod.txt or what ever you named it.

8.5   Editing a Root File

When you open the file browser and you see the Owner of the file is root you must do extra steps to edit that file. Editing some root files can have bad results. Be careful when editing root files. Generally, you can open and view most root files, but they will open in *read only* mode.

8.5.1   The Command Line Way

Open up *Applications > Accessories > Terminal.*

In the terminal window type

```
sudo gedit
```

Open the file with File > Open > Edit

8.5.2   The GUI Way

1. Right click on the desktop and select Create Launcher

2. Type a name in like sudo edit

3. Type *gksudo "gnome-open %u"* as the command and save the launcher to your desktop

4. Drag a file onto your launcher to open and edit

8.5.3   Root Access

In Ubuntu you can become root by typing in "sudo -i" in a terminal window then typing in your password. Be careful, because you can really foul things up as root if you don't know what you're doing.

8.6   Terminal Commands

8.6.1   Working Directory

To find out the path to the present working directory in the terminal window type:

```
pwd
```

8.6.2   Changing Directories

To move up one level in the terminal window type:

```
cd ..
```

To move up two levels in the terminal window type:

```
cd ../..
```

To move down to the emc2/configs subdirectory in the terminal window type:

```
cd emc2/configs
```

8.6.3   Listing files in a directory

To view a list of all the files and subdirectories in the terminal window type:

```
dir
```

or

```
ls
```

8.6.4   Finding a File

The find command can be a bit confusing to a new Linux user. The basic syntax is:

```
find starting-directory parameters actions
```

For example to find all the .ini files in your emc2 directory you first need to use the pwd command to find out the directory.
Open a new terminal window and type:

```
pwd
```

And pwd might return the following result:

```
/home/joe
```

With this information put the command together like this:

```
find /home/joe/linuxcnc -name \*.ini -print
```

The -name is the name of the file your looking for and the -print tells it to print out the result to the terminal window. The *.ini
tells find to return all files that have the .ini extension. The backslash is needed to escape the shell meta-characters. See the find
man page for more information on find.

8.6.5   Searching for Text

```
grep -irl 'text to search for' *
```

This will find all the files that contain the *text to search for* in the current directory and all the subdirectories below it, while
ignoring the case. The -i is for ignore case and the -r is for recursive (include all subdirectories in the search). The -l option will
return a list of the file names, if you leave the -l off you will also get the text where each occourance of the "text to search for" is
found. The * is a wild card for search all files. See the grep man page for more information.

8.6.6 Bootup Messages

To view the bootup messages use "dmesg" from the command window. To save the bootup messages to a file use the redirection operator, like this:

```
dmesg > bootmsg.txt
```

The contents of this file can be copied and pasted on line to share with people trying to help you diagnose your problem.

To clear the message buffer type this:

```
sudo dmesg -c
```

This can be helpful to do just before launching LinuxCNC, so that there will only be a record of information related to the current launch of LinuxCNC.

To find the built in parallel port address use grep to filter the information out of dmesg.

After boot up open a terminal and type:

```
dmesg|grep parport
```

8.7 Convenience Items

8.7.1 Terminal Launcher

If you want to add a terminal launcher to the panel bar on top of the screen you typically can right click on the panel at the top of the screen and select "Add to Panel". Select Custom Application Launcher and Add. Give it a name and put gnome-terminal in the command box.

8.8 Hardware Problems

8.8.1 Hardware Info

To find out what hardware is connected to your motherboard in a terminal window type:

```
lspci -v
```

8.8.2 Monitor Resolution

During installation Ubuntu attempts to detect the monitor settings. If this fails you are left with a generic monitor with a maximum resolution of 800x600.

Instructions for fixing this are located here:

https://help.ubuntu.com/community/FixVideoResolutionHowto

8.9 Paths

Relative Paths Relative paths are based on the startup directory which is the directory containing the ini file. Using relative paths can facilitate relocation of configurations but requires a good understanding of linux path specifiers.

```
./f0        is the same as f0, e.g., a file named f0 in the startup directory
../f1       refers to a file f1 in the parent directory
../../f2    refers to a file f2 in the parent of the parent directory
../../../f3 etc.
```

Chapter 9

Legal Section

9.1 Copyright Terms

Copyright (c) 2000-2013 LinuxCNC.org

Permission is granted to copy, distribute and/or modify this document under the terms of the GNU Free Documentation License, Version 1.1 or any later version published by the Free Software Foundation; with no Invariant Sections, no Front-Cover Texts, and one Back-Cover Text: "This LinuxCNC Handbook is the product of several authors writing for linuxCNC.org. As you find it to be of value in your work, we invite you to contribute to its revision and growth." A copy of the license is included in the section entitled "GNU Free Documentation License". If you do not find the license you may order a copy from Free Software Foundation, Inc. 59 Temple Place, Suite 330, Boston, MA 02111-1307

9.2 GNU Free Documentation License

GNU Free Documentation License Version 1.1, March 2000

Copyright © 2000 Free Software Foundation, Inc. 59 Temple Place, Suite 330, Boston, MA 02111-1307 USA Everyone is permitted to copy and distribute verbatim copies of this license document, but changing it is not allowed.

0. PREAMBLE

The purpose of this License is to make a manual, textbook, or other written document "free" in the sense of freedom: to assure everyone the effective freedom to copy and redistribute it, with or without modifying it, either commercially or noncommercially. Secondarily, this License preserves for the author and publisher a way to get credit for their work, while not being considered responsible for modifications made by others.

This License is a kind of "copyleft", which means that derivative works of the document must themselves be free in the same sense. It complements the GNU General Public License, which is a copyleft license designed for free software.

We have designed this License in order to use it for manuals for free software, because free software needs free documentation: a free program should come with manuals providing the same freedoms that the software does. But this License is not limited to software manuals; it can be used for any textual work, regardless of subject matter or whether it is published as a printed book. We recommend this License principally for works whose purpose is instruction or reference.

1. APPLICABILITY AND DEFINITIONS

This License applies to any manual or other work that contains a notice placed by the copyright holder saying it can be distributed under the terms of this License. The "Document", below, refers to any such manual or work. Any member of the public is a licensee, and is addressed as "you".

A "Modified Version" of the Document means any work containing the Document or a portion of it, either copied verbatim, or with modifications and/or translated into another language.

A "Secondary Section" is a named appendix or a front-matter section of the Document that deals exclusively with the relationship of the publishers or authors of the Document to the Document's overall subject (or to related matters) and contains nothing that could fall directly within that overall subject. (For example, if the Document is in part a textbook of mathematics, a Secondary Section may not explain any mathematics.) The relationship could be a matter of historical connection with the subject or with related matters, or of legal, commercial, philosophical, ethical or political position regarding them.

The "Invariant Sections" are certain Secondary Sections whose titles are designated, as being those of Invariant Sections, in the notice that says that the Document is released under this License.

The "Cover Texts" are certain short passages of text that are listed, as Front-Cover Texts or Back-Cover Texts, in the notice that says that the Document is released under this License.

A "Transparent" copy of the Document means a machine-readable copy, represented in a format whose specification is available to the general public, whose contents can be viewed and edited directly and straightforwardly with generic text editors or (for images composed of pixels) generic paint programs or (for drawings) some widely available drawing editor, and that is suitable for input to text formatters or for automatic translation to a variety of formats suitable for input to text formatters. A copy made in an otherwise Transparent file format whose markup has been designed to thwart or discourage subsequent modification by readers is not Transparent. A copy that is not "Transparent" is called "Opaque".

Examples of suitable formats for Transparent copies include plain ASCII without markup, Texinfo input format, LaTeX input format, SGML or XML using a publicly available DTD, and standard-conforming simple HTML designed for human modification. Opaque formats include PostScript, PDF, proprietary formats that can be read and edited only by proprietary word processors, SGML or XML for which the DTD and/or processing tools are not generally available, and the machine-generated HTML produced by some word processors for output purposes only.

The "Title Page" means, for a printed book, the title page itself, plus such following pages as are needed to hold, legibly, the material this License requires to appear in the title page. For works in formats which do not have any title page as such, "Title Page" means the text near the most prominent appearance of the work's title, preceding the beginning of the body of the text.

2. VERBATIM COPYING

You may copy and distribute the Document in any medium, either commercially or noncommercially, provided that this License, the copyright notices, and the license notice saying this License applies to the Document are reproduced in all copies, and that you add no other conditions whatsoever to those of this License. You may not use technical measures to obstruct or control the reading or further copying of the copies you make or distribute. However, you may accept compensation in exchange for copies. If you distribute a large enough number of copies you must also follow the conditions in section 3.

You may also lend copies, under the same conditions stated above, and you may publicly display copies.

3. COPYING IN QUANTITY

If you publish printed copies of the Document numbering more than 100, and the Document's license notice requires Cover Texts, you must enclose the copies in covers that carry, clearly and legibly, all these Cover Texts: Front-Cover Texts on the front cover, and Back-Cover Texts on the back cover. Both covers must also clearly and legibly identify you as the publisher of these copies. The front cover must present the full title with all words of the title equally prominent and visible. You may add other material on the covers in addition. Copying with changes limited to the covers, as long as they preserve the title of the Document and satisfy these conditions, can be treated as verbatim copying in other respects.

If the required texts for either cover are too voluminous to fit legibly, you should put the first ones listed (as many as fit reasonably) on the actual cover, and continue the rest onto adjacent pages.

If you publish or distribute Opaque copies of the Document numbering more than 100, you must either include a machine-readable Transparent copy along with each Opaque copy, or state in or with each Opaque copy a publicly-accessible computer-network location containing a complete Transparent copy of the Document, free of added material, which the general network-using public has access to download anonymously at no charge using public-standard network protocols. If you use the latter option, you must take reasonably prudent steps, when you begin distribution of Opaque copies in quantity, to ensure that this Transparent copy will remain thus accessible at the stated location until at least one year after the last time you distribute an Opaque copy (directly or through your agents or retailers) of that edition to the public.

It is requested, but not required, that you contact the authors of the Document well before redistributing any large number of copies, to give them a chance to provide you with an updated version of the Document.

4. MODIFICATIONS

You may copy and distribute a Modified Version of the Document under the conditions of sections 2 and 3 above, provided that you release the Modified Version under precisely this License, with the Modified Version filling the role of the Document, thus licensing distribution and modification of the Modified Version to whoever possesses a copy of it. In addition, you must do these things in the Modified Version:

A. Use in the Title Page (and on the covers, if any) a title distinct from that of the Document, and from those of previous versions (which should, if there were any, be listed in the History section of the Document). You may use the same title as a previous version if the original publisher of that version gives permission. B. List on the Title Page, as authors, one or more persons or entities responsible for authorship of the modifications in the Modified Version, together with at least five of the principal authors of the Document (all of its principal authors, if it has less than five). C. State on the Title page the name of the publisher of the Modified Version, as the publisher. D. Preserve all the copyright notices of the Document. E. Add an appropriate copyright notice for your modifications adjacent to the other copyright notices. F. Include, immediately after the copyright notices, a license notice giving the public permission to use the Modified Version under the terms of this License, in the form shown in the Addendum below. G. Preserve in that license notice the full lists of Invariant Sections and required Cover Texts given in the Document's license notice. H. Include an unaltered copy of this License. I. Preserve the section entitled "History", and its title, and add to it an item stating at least the title, year, new authors, and publisher of the Modified Version as given on the Title Page. If there is no section entitled "History" in the Document, create one stating the title, year, authors, and publisher of the Document as given on its Title Page, then add an item describing the Modified Version as stated in the previous sentence. J. Preserve the network location, if any, given in the Document for public access to a Transparent copy of the Document, and likewise the network locations given in the Document for previous versions it was based on. These may be placed in the "History" section. You may omit a network location for a work that was published at least four years before the Document itself, or if the original publisher of the version it refers to gives permission. K. In any section entitled "Acknowledgements" or "Dedications", preserve the section's title, and preserve in the section all the substance and tone of each of the contributor acknowledgements and/or dedications given therein. L. Preserve all the Invariant Sections of the Document, unaltered in their text and in their titles. Section numbers or the equivalent are not considered part of the section titles. M. Delete any section entitled "Endorsements". Such a section may not be included in the Modified Version. N. Do not retitle any existing section as "Endorsements" or to conflict in title with any Invariant Section.

If the Modified Version includes new front-matter sections or appendices that qualify as Secondary Sections and contain no material copied from the Document, you may at your option designate some or all of these sections as invariant. To do this, add their titles to the list of Invariant Sections in the Modified Version's license notice. These titles must be distinct from any other section titles.

You may add a section entitled "Endorsements", provided it contains nothing but endorsements of your Modified Version by various parties—for example, statements of peer review or that the text has been approved by an organization as the authoritative definition of a standard.

You may add a passage of up to five words as a Front-Cover Text, and a passage of up to 25 words as a Back-Cover Text, to the end of the list of Cover Texts in the Modified Version. Only one passage of Front-Cover Text and one of Back-Cover Text may be added by (or through arrangements made by) any one entity. If the Document already includes a cover text for the same cover, previously added by you or by arrangement made by the same entity you are acting on behalf of, you may not add another; but you may replace the old one, on explicit permission from the previous publisher that added the old one.

The author(s) and publisher(s) of the Document do not by this License give permission to use their names for publicity for or to assert or imply endorsement of any Modified Version.

5. COMBINING DOCUMENTS

You may combine the Document with other documents released under this License, under the terms defined in section 4 above for modified versions, provided that you include in the combination all of the Invariant Sections of all of the original documents, unmodified, and list them all as Invariant Sections of your combined work in its license notice.

The combined work need only contain one copy of this License, and multiple identical Invariant Sections may be replaced with a single copy. If there are multiple Invariant Sections with the same name but different contents, make the title of each such section unique by adding at the end of it, in parentheses, the name of the original author or publisher of that section if known, or else a unique number. Make the same adjustment to the section titles in the list of Invariant Sections in the license notice of the combined work.

In the combination, you must combine any sections entitled "History" in the various original documents, forming one section entitled "History"; likewise combine any sections entitled "Acknowledgements", and any sections entitled "Dedications". You must delete all sections entitled "Endorsements."

6. COLLECTIONS OF DOCUMENTS

You may make a collection consisting of the Document and other documents released under this License, and replace the individual copies of this License in the various documents with a single copy that is included in the collection, provided that you follow the rules of this License for verbatim copying of each of the documents in all other respects.

You may extract a single document from such a collection, and distribute it individually under this License, provided you insert a copy of this License into the extracted document, and follow this License in all other respects regarding verbatim copying of that document.

7. AGGREGATION WITH INDEPENDENT WORKS

A compilation of the Document or its derivatives with other separate and independent documents or works, in or on a volume of a storage or distribution medium, does not as a whole count as a Modified Version of the Document, provided no compilation copyright is claimed for the compilation. Such a compilation is called an "aggregate", and this License does not apply to the other self-contained works thus compiled with the Document, on account of their being thus compiled, if they are not themselves derivative works of the Document.

If the Cover Text requirement of section 3 is applicable to these copies of the Document, then if the Document is less than one quarter of the entire aggregate, the Document's Cover Texts may be placed on covers that surround only the Document within the aggregate. Otherwise they must appear on covers around the whole aggregate.

8. TRANSLATION

Translation is considered a kind of modification, so you may distribute translations of the Document under the terms of section 4. Replacing Invariant Sections with translations requires special permission from their copyright holders, but you may include translations of some or all Invariant Sections in addition to the original versions of these Invariant Sections. You may include a translation of this License provided that you also include the original English version of this License. In case of a disagreement between the translation and the original English version of this License, the original English version will prevail.

9. TERMINATION

You may not copy, modify, sublicense, or distribute the Document except as expressly provided for under this License. Any other attempt to copy, modify, sublicense or distribute the Document is void, and will automatically terminate your rights under this License. However, parties who have received copies, or rights, from you under this License will not have their licenses terminated so long as such parties remain in full compliance.

10. FUTURE REVISIONS OF THIS LICENSE

The Free Software Foundation may publish new, revised versions of the GNU Free Documentation License from time to time. Such new versions will be similar in spirit to the present version, but may differ in detail to address new problems or concerns. See http://www.gnu.org/copyleft/.

Each version of the License is given a distinguishing version number. If the Document specifies that a particular numbered version of this License "or any later version" applies to it, you have the option of following the terms and conditions either of that specified version or of any later version that has been published (not as a draft) by the Free Software Foundation. If the Document does not specify a version number of this License, you may choose any version ever published (not as a draft) by the Free Software Foundation.

ADDENDUM: How to use this License for your documents

To use this License in a document you have written, include a copy of the License in the document and put the following copyright and license notices just after the title page:

Copyright (c) YEAR YOUR NAME. Permission is granted to copy, distribute and/or modify this document under the terms of the GNU Free Documentation License, Version 1.1 or any later version published by the Free Software Foundation; with the Invariant Sections being LIST THEIR TITLES, with the Front-Cover Texts being LIST, and with the Back-Cover Texts being LIST. A copy of the license is included in the section entitled "GNU Free Documentation License".

If you have no Invariant Sections, write "with no Invariant Sections" instead of saying which ones are invariant. If you have no Front-Cover Texts, write "no Front-Cover Texts" instead of "Front-Cover Texts being LIST"; likewise for Back-Cover Texts.

If your document contains nontrivial examples of program code, we recommend releasing these examples in parallel under your choice of free software license, such as the GNU General Public License, to permit their use in free software.

Chapter 10

Index